Leading
Turnaround Teams

By Gene Wood
and
Daniel Harkavy

St. Charles, IL 60174
1-800-253-4276

Published by ChurchSmart Resources

We are an evangelical Christian publisher committed to producing excellent products at affordable prices to help church leaders accomplish effective ministry in the areas of Church planting, Church growth, Church renewal and Leadership development.

For a free catalog of our resources call 1-800-253-4276.
Visit us at: www.churchsmart.com

Cover design by: Julie Becker

Manuscript edited by: Stuart Hoffman

© copyright 2004
 by Gene Wood

ISBN#: 1-889638-46-3

Leading
Turnaround Teams

ACKNOWLEDGEMENTS

Gene Wood

I wish to express my appreciation to the teams, who are content to play the game of life with me. Together we have experienced so many wins. I fully anticipate the greatest days are ahead. I say thank you to:

Carol my wife of 28 years. You've been the ultimate team player. You're too seldom noticed but all of us on this team know who deserves credit for any success we've enjoyed. I've often shared with others that I suspect when I die you will want my heart because you probably think I've never used it. Fortunately you bring enough heart to the game for both of us.

The leadership team of Grace Church. Few pastors will ever be privileged to work alongside a board and staff modeling the blends of competency and humility; leadership and meekness; grace and truth as you have. You make writing a book on team building very easy.

Our congregational team. You have done the work of the ministry. You have given sacrificially and cheerfully. You have followed your leaders when we could not fully explain all we were asking for. Your trust and labors of love have allowed us to enjoy 11 consecutive years of growth. It is a joy to serve you.

Daniel Harkavy

My wife and mate for life, Sheri. You are the best friend and encourager I could ever ask for. My incredible children, Allie, Dylan, wesley and Emily. God created you for very special purposes and I honored to be your father. I love you!

The awesome team of sold our champions that I get to spend my days with at Building Champions and Ministry Coaching International. Your convictions and commitment spur me on!

My Band of Brothers abroad. Thanks for covering my back and being men of faith, love and courage. Your questions, encouragement, challenges, life examples and friendship keep my humble.

To all those that have devoted their lives to leading His flock. I pray for you and thank you for doing what He has called you to do.

CONTENTS

INTRODUCTION

What is Leading Turnaround All About?

By Gene Wood

S urprised. This is the word that summarizes how I feel about the reception to *Leading Turnaround Churches*, first published in 2001. I wrote from the perspective of a white, Conservative Baptist, middle-class American. I just assumed that the readership would come from that narrow slice of pie. Was I ever wrong! In fact, leaders from over 22 different denominations have shown interest.

I was even more flabbergasted when seminars were requested from other countries. *LTC* has already been printed in South Korea and the Philippines. Seminars have also been hosted in Canada.

Local churches around the world have more in common than they have in distinction. To paraphrase 1 Corinthians 10:13: "Your local church is not having difficulties and challenges which are not also being experienced by the church 10, 100, or 1,000 miles away.

TWO KEY STATISTICS

When writing *LTC*, I seized upon a couple of statistics and decided to run with them. I thought that if they were way off base, I'd be corrected and could simply apologize.

The first statistic is that 70 − 85 percent of all local Protestant churches are experiencing plateau or decline. I have now BETA tested the premise with state, regional and national leaders from the 22 denominations. *None* of them has argued that this statistic does *not* apply to the group they oversee. Because of the breadth of groups represented — World Wide Church of God, Conservative Baptist, Free Methodists, Southern Baptists, Lutheran Church Missouri Synod, Evangelical Friends, American Baptists, Church of God, Assemblies of God, etc. — this constitutes a rather convincing argument.

I believe pastors are basically good people. Most of them are fun loving, hard working, and quite anxious to get along with those they serve. They have tried everything within their power to help the churches they serve. As a group, they are peacemakers, willing to listen and work through relational tensions. To sum up pastors: they are *nice.* So if simply being nice were the solution to having healthier churches, we would not have the dismal situation we now face.

Seventy to eighty-five percent! One study clearly shows that between 1976 and 1986 the American population grew by 11 percent, while church attendance decreased by 9 percent. If that trend continues, the Protestant church will be virtually nonexistent in five decades. Being nice is not working. If we always do what we've always done, we'll always get what we've always got. I'm not making an appeal for mean-spirited leadership. But we must call out for strong and effective leadership! Appeasement of unreasonable and nonproductive behavior in our churches must end.

The second statistic presented in *LTC* is the 95 percent theory. That is, 95 percent of all major problems in the local church are basically a power struggle. Someone asked me where I got that figure. My response was to tell them that 89.3 percent of all statistics are made up on the spot—including this one.

Ninety-five percent is a figure of speech implying that most of the major problems in church that prevent growth and health are the result of power issues. Other matters are usually worked out or overcome in some way. Power struggles, however, are fundamentally irresolvable because they involve two questions. The first is "In what direction are we heading?" The second is "Who made that decision?" Ultimately someone must lead, and someone may have to leave.

WHERE IS THIS HEADED?

As I teach the two-day LTC seminar, I have been startled at the contrasting questions asked. Toward the end of the first day, in which we discuss the unhealthy condition of the North American church and the obstacles to growth (bucket brigades and "those who cannot leave"), I stress how essential it is for pastors to confront these issues and remove the roadblocks to becoming a healthy church.

Invariably someone will ask, "Gene, what can pastors do if they are not a SNL [strong natural leader]? Most of our pastors are caregivers and nonconfrontive. What you are suggesting requires a hard-driving, type A personality. So what about the rest of us?"

Or they comment: "Gene, you seem to suggest that the pastor is *the* leader. What about equipping and working with a team of people?"

By the end of day two, I frequently hear something to this effect: "Gene it sounds as if the pastor is not the one who casts the vision. All the emphasis you place upon group decisions regarding the master plan and goals of the church seems to make the voice of the pastor just one of many. Isn't the pastor supposed to lead?"

I share that to build effective churches there is a crucial need to develop ownership from the team of leaders and eventually from the entire congregation. A leader can make all the decisions in the church *if* he or she can pay all the bills in the church. For almost two years I would stop and allow that statement to sink in and then ask seminar participants rhetorically, "Is there anyone here who can pay all the bills in their church?" No one ever raised his or her hand — until a seminar in South Korea. Very timidly, but sincerely, a sweet-appearing woman raised her hand. Evidently there are some leaders in the world who have the financial capability to pay all the bills, but that would certainly hinder developing committed disciples of Christ were they to be robbed of the joy of stewardship.

Thesis of Leading Turnaround Teams

"Turnaround begins with leadership but will be implemented through teamwork."

Obviously the term *lead* must mean something. It is listed as a spiritual gift. Most every church affirms the need for it. On the other hand, healthy churches rate high on "empowering leadership." In what areas must the pastor take responsibility, and when should he allow consensus among the team to rule the day? Excellent leaders do not make many decisions, but they know which decisions they must make. They are both autocratic and laissez faire, consensus builders and authoritarian. See the chart below. In what matters of church life should a pastor display each of the various approaches to leadership?

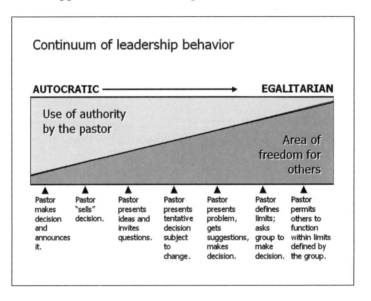

The ability to provide strong leadership while steadily increasing the number of supporters for the vision is a major factor in whether the turn-around will ultimately prove successful. Truly effective leaders build strong teams that both shape and implement the organizational vision.

Assumptions of Leading Turnaround Teams

1. Strong leadership is biblical. Teamwork is biblical.

2. Leadership and teams are not mutually exclusive, they are comple-mentary.

3. Every effective team knows who its leader is.

4. The readers of LTT will be leaders in churches averaging less than 400 in attendance in morning worship and those responsible for their care and development.

5. Leaders must do what only the leader can effectively do and teams must do what teams do best.

While a student in seminary, I taught at Southern Bible Institute. Founded by Harry Ironside, this school has provided valuable training for African American pastors in the Dallas/Fort Worth area who, due to either schedules or finances, were unable to attend an accredited college. Dr. Reed was dean of students during those years. One day the subject of leadership in the church came up. I'll never forget what he said: "You know, if you were to go out in your back yard, and your dog had two heads, you'd shoot that thing. That's no dog—it's a monster." His observation prompted me to think about organisms and heads. As best I can see, everything God created has only one head. Why should a church be any different?

What Is Coaching All About?

By Daniel Harkavy

Coaching is no longer just for athletes and performers. It is one of the fastest growing professions in America. The United Coaching Federation states that there are more than 10,000 coaches practicing today. Coaching is now making its way into the church as well.

The role of pastor is one of the most challenging and lonely leadership positions in the world. You're called by God to look out for His sheep; you're expected to have a red phone on your desk that is a direct line to Him for all of life's answers; you're expected to respond to every member's needs and hurts, becks and calls; you're to be available 24/7, to motivate and inspire us several times per week; to be growing in Him; to be above reproach; to skillfully lead your fellow teammates and a staff of volunteers; to raise sufficient funds for growth; to live like a pauper; to be strong, sympathetic, merciful, and compassionate; to masterfully lead your board; and, in your spare time, keep *your* family affairs in order! **Yikes**! How would Jesus handle this job? Some pastors are finding great assistance with the help of a coach.

Coaching is all about:

- ◆ Relationships

- ◆ Direction

- ◆ Encouragement

- ◆ Exhortation

- Accountability

- Communication

- Listening

- Feedback

- Clarity

- Removing roadblocks and hurdles

- Identifying opportunities

- Tapping into skills and gifts that need to be honed

- Identifying priorities

- Breaking down projects into manageable chunks

- Helping to define roles and priorities

As the great NFL coach Tom Landry puts it, "A coach is someone who tells you what you don't want to hear, and has you see what you don't want to see, so you can be who you have always known you can be."

A Great Coach:

1. Is brutally honest

2. Is a big-picture thinker

3. Is motivated by causing others to succeed; does not need to be on the center stage

4. Has strong convictions and principles about what constitutes success and has values that are congruent with yours

5. Listens, thinks, and then speaks with clarity

6. Will commit time to you regularly

7. Bonus: Has years of experience doing what you do

What will a coach do for me?

Good coaches will do five things to guarantee your continued growth:

1. Create awareness: They will cause you to evaluate yourself and your organization at a level that hits you at your core. If you don't truly know where you are and how you got there, moving forward will be a struggle full of uncertainty and fear.

2. Help you develop a vision: What will your church look like and be known for five to ten years from now? Do you know? If not, getting out of the day-to-day routine of leading your team and church will be next to impossible. If done right, this will put that fire back in your belly and cause you to wake up daily with a new excitement and passion.

3. Help you to develop a plan: This plan begins with your vision, moves to your goals, and then focuses on the annual, quarterly, monthly, weekly, and daily activities that will enable your vision to become a reality.

4. Keep you on the plan: They will provide you with inspiration and accountability. A good coach will keep you focused on both the vision and the right daily activities so you progress with success and balance. They will not allow you to stray too far before they pull you back on track.

5. Help you process your thoughts: They will challenge you and act as sounding boards and brainstorming partners so you can stretch and make quantum leap decisions.

Would I benefit from being coached?

I believe coaching can help all of us in many different areas of our careers and our lives. Jim Rohn says In *Leading an Inspired Life*, "Accepting responsibility is one of the highest forms of human maturity. It is a willingness to be accountable, to put yourself on the line. It is really the defining characteristic of adulthood." At a seminar I recently attended, one of the many gems I heard was that if I am to continue learning, I must be a student of myself. In other words, I need to study my strengths, my weakness, my desires, and my fears and then plan accordingly.

Once this is done, I will have greater success if I have someone on my team who is committed to seeing me succeed. One who is not afraid to tell me when I am off course. One who is charged up about being part of my improvement and success. This can be a humbling process and yet is so powerful if the time, format, and coach are right for you.

Ask yourself these five questions before you spend time in a coaching relationship:

1. Do I believe I can grow?

2. Do I want someone knowing what makes me tick?

3. Do I want someone keeping me focused and on task?

4. Do I want to submit to another person's ideas, directions, and leadership?

5. Am I truly prepared to invest the money and time to think, plan, study, and practice in order to get my life, church, and team to the next level?

If you answered yes to all of the above questions, having a qualified coach on your team is a must. If you are uncertain about any of the above questions, take some time praying and thinking about where you are today versus where you thought you would be today one year ago. Think about where you are going and if you are equipped to get there. A serious desire for improvement and accountability is essential if one is to truly benefit from being coached.

Being coached is an incredible experience. Having an individual on your team whose primary objective is to help you grow as a leader and succeed in your calling and life should prove to be invaluable.

Who is Daniel Harkavy?

What would you say if I were to tell you I had a deal for you? I'll let you talk to a friend of mine every other week over the phone for 30 minutes for the next 12 months. It will only cost you $9,000. But, for the privilege of doing so, you must agree to do all the homework assignments he gives you and follow through with all commitments you make during those phone conversations. Well, that is what many of the nation's most successful business leaders are doing when they contract Daniel Harkavy to coach them.

In *Leading Turnaround Teams* you will be the first to receive his valuable leadership coaching tips in the nonprofit sector. Please don't underestimate how his counsel, insights, and suggestions can radically change your life for the better. But they must be acted on. Intention must be followed by implementation.

Wally and Gloria invited us to their lovely home shortly after we arrived in Glendora, California. Gloria had been one of the search committee members responsible for our call. We were impressed with their character, hospitality, and warmth, so were not surprised to find many of the same characteristics in their daughter, Sheri and son-in-law, Daniel. This was my introduction to Daniel Harkavy.

At that time, he and his wife were the poster couple for California cool. They had just purchased a new home. Daniel surfed and played the drums. He oozed confidence, dressed well, and for a young man in his twenties, was obviously doing well in the mortgage business. Sheri rolled her eyes at some of his outrageous comments, but it was apparent she deeply admired him.

Frankly, Daniel was still a little rough around the edges; he needed some polishing. In this book he will tell you some of that story. But from the first time I met him, I sensed he was a winner. The only question was whether he would choose to win only for himself and his family or would he step outside that small circle and become a winner for the larger community and, ultimately, for God.

In his early 30s Daniel decided to take a sabbatical and move to Oregon with his growing family. Before he left, I felt compelled to invite him to join me for lunch with Don Modglin, one of my heroes. Don was also a businessperson. God blessed him financially many years ago as he worked in the banking industry. Don and his wife have committed to use their resources for the good of others and the sake of the Lord by creating the Modglin Family Foundation.

As we drove away from the luncheon, I said to Daniel, "You and Sheri are not where the Modglins are yet, but I believe you will be someday. Remember, the measure of a successful man is how much he can give away, not how much he can keep. I just wanted you to meet someone who is making wise and lasting life investments."

Daniel moved to Lake Oswego, Oregon. We talked from time to time over the phone. Eventually he decided to go back to work. He developed a company called Building Champions. At that time I was serving as national spokesperson for our denomination. I invited Daniel and Sheri to join us for a donor luncheon we were hosting in Phoenix, Arizona. I wanted to help implant a visual image in their minds of what can happen when people with significant resources come together and share a common vision.

Years later I was overjoyed when Daniel invited me to join him at the Building Champions headquarters to sit and talk about his vision for coaching ministry leaders. Few with his talents, intuitive grasp for good decisions, work ethic, physical attributes (he works out and runs marathons), gift of gab, and ability to make money seem to be able to recognize that all they possess is in the end a stewardship, that is, a responsibility to give back. This awareness, I believe, is what will continue to set Daniel Harkavy apart from the pack.

Just two weeks ago Daniel shared that he had brought a small circle of friends and clients together and they had committed close to $500,000 for their pastoral coaching ministry, Ministry Coaching International. Daniel understands the responsibility of influence.

I believe in Daniel Harkavy. I believe he understands life-coaching as well as anyone. I believe he is sincere in all he does. I believe he is going to finish the race well. I believe he is bigger than himself.

It is a joy to coauthor this work with him. You will likely hear his name often in the years ahead. Someone reminded me recently that while you can count the seeds in an apple, you cannot count the apples in a seed. I am confident Daniel's life will result in immeasurable fruit for the kingdom.

Gene Wood
Glendora, CA
April 2004

Who is Gene Wood?

It was a weeknight in December of 1990. My wife Sheri and I had just made our first move from one church to another as a married couple. We were twenty-six and were trying out the church in which she had grown up: Grace Baptist Church, Glendora. My in-laws, Wally and Gloria Howard, were involved with the leadership of the church and were on the pastoral search committee. They asked us to join them for dinner to meet their most promising pastoral candidate and his family. I was maybe about three years into my journey with Christ and had had only a handful of personal conversations with a pastor. Out of obligation, I accepted the dinner invitation and showed up to meet this pastor and his holy family. I was sure that this night would be a sleeper. What would we talk about? I was young and very immature in my walk. My world was still my focus. We sat down for dinner and I saw this surprisingly normal family interact. I observed how Gene communicated with his wonderful wife and very mature and bright kids. By the end of the night, I knew that if the Wood family made the move to lead our church, I would personally benefit. He was a genuine man, and that night I made a connection with him.

Gene accepted the position as Senior Pastor. Over the next year, he and I met several times and he truly challenged me in my faith and knowledge. His sermons were awe inspiring. He made the Bible come to life and increased my desire to study it on my own. Sheri and I attended a Sunday school class for young married couples. I hooked up with some other young men, and we started a men's study. My heart was beginning to be transformed. I was no longer just a Sunday Christian.

Shortly after I was baptized, Pastor Gene asked me if I would be willing to share my testimony on a Sunday morning. This was a difficult request for me because I had grown up in this area and was not known for being a godly person. Getting up in front of the church felt very unnatural and risky. I was nervous and weak in the knees, but I told my story.

Two weeks later I got the call. Pastor Gene wanted to have breakfast with me. We met at a local restaurant and ordered our meals. I asked Gene the purpose of our meeting.

"Daniel, you are going to want to finish your breakfast before we discuss this." OK, I thought with my heart dropping to my stomach. I made some small talk and ate as fast as I could. Then came the punch to the gut. He told me that the day after I gave my testimony, a young couple made an appointment to see him. They told him that if people like me were going to be involved with the leadership of the church, they would be moving on. The young woman was a coworker of a high school friend of mine, had heard stories of my wild behavior and related to pastor Gene some of the graphic details.

Gene asked me the most direct and embarrassing question I have ever been asked. I was stunned, certain that my relationship with Pastor Gene was over and that I would have to leave that church. How could my pre-Christian behavior ruin what presently seemed to be going so well?

I apologized to Gene and then called the young couple to apologize to them. I assured them that I was no longer that same party animal. Christ was transforming me: He was doing a work in me. All of them were very gracious and forgiving.

My dear friend, Pastor Gene Wood, helped teach me some huge lessons at this difficult breakfast meeting.

Lesson One: Every small stupid decision you make helps build your reputation, and they can follow you for years.

Lesson Two: A real leader cares enough to ask the difficult questions.

Lesson Three: A turnaround pastor turns the church around by turning its members around. This encounter with Gene was the beginning of a turnaround in my life.

Lesson Four: You never know who is watching you and who will talk about you. Paul challenges us in 1 Corinthians 9:27 to beat our body and make it our slave so that after we have preached we may not be disqualified. Do not let your actions disqualify you from building His kingdom.

Lesson Five: Jesus came to seek and save sinners and set the captives free. Amen.

A few years later, Pastor Gene taught our congregation a huge lesson in leadership. He was building momentum within the church and with his pastoral team. Satan took notice and unleashed his force on a young pastor and his family. Pastor Gene did not allow a week to pass before he dealt with this head on. In a Sunday service he let the congregation know that sin had entered into our church leadership team and exactly how he was dealing with it. He let us know what we needed to know and then strongly encouraged us to not participate in the sin by talking about it, gossiping, or sticking our noses where they did not belong. The young couple repented, and their marriage was healed. They are well and active today in church leadership. This could have been devastating not only to the couple, but to the members of the church body if it would have been handled in any other manner.

I had the wonderful opportunity to join Gene on a board and serve as an advisor to him when he was involved at a national level with his denomination. I had always respected him as a leader and I fully enjoyed colaboring with him as a lay leader. Here I saw how Gene's passion and vision for the church were bigger than our church congregation in Glendora. In 1999 God had laid on my heart the desire to take the business coaching systems and skills that we had developed at Building Champions and offer them to pastors.

I wanted to make sure that I was on track with this opportunity, so I asked my closest advisors and friends to join me in an all-day vision-casting and strategic planning session. Gene was one of the 23 men there. Many of them contributed with affirmations and great insights as to how we should structure this offering.

Gene took a different approach. He wanted to make sure we were not missing any of the potential hurdles or roadblocks. He brought up some serious concerns, and, though he took some heat that day, I knew his heart and found his input to be incredibly valuable. As a result, Building His Champions, which is now Ministry Coaching International, was born. It has been such a privilege to coach pastors and ministry leaders to new levels of success as they lead their churches, teams, and homes.

I tend to be overly optimistic and have a strong ability to influence. Because of these traits I can usually sell any group on my ideas and plans. As we all know, our greatest strengths can also be our greatest weaknesses. Knowing this about myself, I value those friends and advisors who have the courage to really question and challenge my ideas and motives. I think this is why we are instructed in Proverbs to gather counsel in order to prevent our plans from failing. Over the years Gene has consistently given me wise counsel.

What has impressed me most about Gene, and what causes me to call him a "dear friend," is his heart for Christ. Gene lives Colossians 1:28-29 and is a soldout laborer for the kingdom. His heart for the church and for us as its members is evident in everything he is and does. I count it a great privilege to partner with him on this book; my hope is that he will have the same impact on you that he has had on me.

Now some of you who are saying, "Great. Another turnaround book by Gene Wood ... but who is this Daniel S. Harkavy and how will he relate to me?" Great question. Everything that I contributed to this book came as a result of God allowing me to be involved in the lives of hundreds, if not thousands, of leaders over the years. One of the greatest benefits that have come from coaching others is what they have taught me in the process. So I glean my perspectives from seven areas.

They are:

- My own leadership experiences

- Coaching business leaders

- Coaching our team of coaches at Building Champions and Ministry Coaching International

- Spending time with dear friends that pastor churches

- Serving as the chair of the board at Ministry Coaching International and being connected to some of the finest pastoral coaches in the world

- Serving as an elder at our home church

- Praying for huge wisdom as I worked with Gene to write this book

I have never been a pastor, nor do I really know exactly what it's like to be in your shoes. I hope that my heart, coaching, and business experiences will in some way speak to you in a way that encourages and instructs you how to better live out your wonderful calling.

Daniel Harkavy
Lake Oswego, OR
April 2004

CHAPTER 1

Convictions

By Gene Wood

Go to any local book store. Check the Internet. How many books written during the past 15 years talk about convictions? Volumes have been turned out that discuss values, vision, purpose, passion, and mission. But what can you find on convictions?

One thesis of this book is that effective teams must begin with convictions. These convictions must be brought to the team by the leader. They cannot be developed by a group.

Let's look at this more closely in the context of the local church. While the principles of this book can be applied to religious nonprofit organizations besides the local church, this book will focus on local churches. Following are our assumptions regarding the local church and its leadership:

1. Everything rises and falls with leadership.

2. The pastor is the logical functional leader in a local church.

3. Every organization must clearly understand who the leader is.

4. The pastor-leader brings the core convictions to the team.

5. If the core convictions of the organization cannot be aligned with the leader, the leader must be changed.

6. Denial of any of the above assumptions will create chaos in the church.

Let's begin by distinguishing values from convictions:

Values	Convictions
Will commit to . . .	Will sacrifice for . . .
Will contemplate the cost of . . .	No cost is too great . . .
Are negotiable . . .	Non-negotiable . . .
Ask others to subscribe . . .	Expect/demand others to subscribe . . .
Decided by the group . . .	Decided by the individual . . .
For a season . . .	For a lifetime . . .
Can be changed by vote . . .	Cannot be changed . . .
External compliance acceptable . . .	Internal ownership essential . . .
Can be political . . .	Never political . . .
Can remain if changes . . .	Cannot remain if changes . . .

One reason we hear so much about values today versus convictions in the church is that church leadership has borrowed so heavily from the business model. If you study the above list, it will become quickly apparent that *no* business can or even does have convictions as described above. Their values may be high and lofty, but convictions are the sole domain of an overtly religious organization which discovers what is right and wrong from a sacred revelation that is not subject to change.

Convictions are not terribly popular today. However, a number of writers have begun to raise their voices for convictions. In the 1970s Dean Kelly, himself a member of a liberal church group, wrote a book titled *Why Conservative Churches Are Growing*. It is a must read, even 30 years later. Thom Rainer has done an excellent job of documenting the value of convictions in his recent book, *High Expectation Churches*, and Willard Erickson's *The Evangelical Left* has shown the undesirable results of evangelical groups that have attempted to become all things to all people. While these authors do not specifically use the word *convictions*, that is essentially what they are speaking of.

Our plea to all church, mission, and denominational leaders is to consider the value of reinstituting clear convictions into the life of their organizations. We could argue that this should be done for practical reasons of survival even if personal convictions are not held, but that is not possible.

Either leaders have convictions or they do not. That is why it is so essential for those responsible for hiring the leader to consider this issue seriously. The health, and even the survival, of the organization may be determined ultimately by the strength of the convictions on the part of the pastor or leader who is called.

In LTC (Leading Turnaround Churches) seminars, we have worked with leaders from more than 22 various denominations. Often I have pled with them to lead out of conviction. If you are Lutheran—be a good Lutheran. If you are a member of the Assembly of God—be a good member of that church. If you are Free Methodist—be a good Free Methodist. If you are a Baptist—be a good Baptist. We owe it to our constituency and to the world to wave our Bibles and declare with certainty, "Thus says the Lord."

In areas of disagreement, we cannot all be correct. Logic dictates that we may all be wrong, but we cannot all be right. That fact, however, should not prevent leaders from boldly declaring where they stand and explaining why. Of course, this boldness will mean that they will lose some members. But those who follow will do so with confidence and reassurance.

Upon our arrival at Grace Church in Glendora, I was quickly confronted by members with an appeal to be sensitive and kind to an elderly gentleman who had just been accepted into membership in the church. They explained that Bill (not his real name) was a good man. He did not, however, believe Jesus was God. He maintained that Jesus was the son of God, but not actually God. A few people wanted to make sure I would not make him feel uncomfortable. They explained he was an emotionally fragile man and could suffer great emotional trauma if dealt with too severely. I told my wife not to unpack the rest of our boxes. For, if this issue were not resolved, we would not be at Grace very long.

Whatever your position may be on this matter, you will certainly see that a church cannot believe Jesus is God and that He also may not be fully God. This was basically a question of conviction and leadership. The implications were significant. Our church needed to decide where we stood. We did speak with the gentleman and informed him of our convictions. After listening, he decided to withdraw his membership.

This contemporary perspective, which seemingly declares the church today can be certain of very little, is confusing our nation. If leaders are not sure what the Bible teaches, then how can members have confidence that the Word of God is adequate for correction, for instruction, and for living a confident life?

The doctrine of perspicuity of Scripture is a lost teaching. Historically, the church has held that the Word of God is not only accurate and trustworthy, but it is also clear and can be understood. If we lose this, we have little to separate us from society that is lost in the swamp of ambiguity and uncertainty.

Two factors have converged to make this topic one that we fear to address.

1. Pressure of post-modernity. The bottom line of this wave of thinking is that A can equal non-A. Therefore, while I may be correct in what I believe, I cannot say with confidence that others are wrong, even if their belief is diametrically opposite of the truth I hold sacred. In essence, everyone is correct. A mission leader once looked at me boldly and proudly declared, "We are not against anything here." He was attempting to communicate a loving and tolerant attitude that he hoped characterized the mission he leads, but the statement should send shock waves through any thinking person with convictions. The basic question is whether the Old Testament prophets, the apostles, and Jesus were "against" anything. Even a cursory reading of Scripture reveals numerous examples of negative, critical thinking by godly people.

   Graciousness should typify our demeanor and humility clothe our understanding. However, that does not mitigate the responsibility of leaders to boldly declare that if there is some body of information called truth, then there is logically a body of teaching we must declare error.

2. Recent political events have caused the concept of "fundamentalism" to fall on hard times. Fundamentalism basically declares that there is absolute truth worth dying for. In such areas of truth, all others are wrong. The truth cannot be compromised and even dialogue can be dangerous.

GREAT LEADERS

For each of the past six years, some pastors and their spouses have visited a different great church leader. We spend two days with these leaders to learn from them and their experiences. A few of those we have met with include John McArthur, Leith Anderson, Eddie Dobson, Adrian Rogers, and Jack Graham. Each is a mega-church leader who has enjoyed unusual success by any standard of measurement. Each is committed to biblical truth and is a man of exceptional character.

If we were to put all of these great pastor-leaders together in a small room and ask them to discuss philosophy of ministry and methodology, it would make for a fascinating and probably heated debate. The differences of opinion would be great. None of them would back down. Each is 100 percent committed to the way they "do church."

Each believes that the way he does church is the best and that his interpretation of Scripture is the correct one. Each has a determination and strategy to train those who come to his church to believe as he does. That is what leadership-conviction does.

Great churches are always founded on the shoulders of great leaders. And great leaders always have personal convictions that cannot be shaken.

Some may point out that there are other ecclesiastical leaders with far more open positions. This is true. A well-known example would be Dr. Robert Schuller. He is quite tolerant and open to theological diversity. But that simply reflects his conviction to openness and tolerance. His convictions are still solid and unchanging. He has stood by them in the face of much criticism.

A CLOSING WORD

What do you believe? What are you willing to be fired for? What nonnegotiable beliefs do you as a leader bring to the organization you lead? Until you can answer these questions, it is unlikely many will be inspired to follow you and sacrifice to make your dream a reality.

At Grace Church we spend one half of our new member sessions talking about convictions. We explain who we are as a church and what will be expected of you if you choose to join. I tell prospective members that I know how I could help grow our church faster. However, I explain, that is not our goal; our goal is "to glorify God by developing committed followers of Jesus Christ who attract others to Him." I share openly the areas where we are narrower than other churches (I prefer to think of it as what makes us unique). I explain that there are many churches in our area they can join, and that we cannot be all things to all people.

After each new members class, some choose to look elsewhere. But those who join us know who we are and what we believe. The result has been ten straight years of growth. It is healthier to take the slow quarter than the fast nickel. How can any organization grow on a shaky foundation? When we grow with people who either do not fully understand what we believe or are not fully committed to what we believe, we will experience half-hearted commitment and steady erosion.

Leaders are paid for doing very little. But one thing they must do is bring convictions to the table.

CHAPTER 2

Commitment

By Gene Wood

C ommitment also must be brought to the church by the pastor before an effective team can be built. This commitment involves the "where" and "what" of ministry. Without this dynamic brought by the leader, there will be perpetual uncertainty, fear, and mistrust.

1. Commitment to the Calling

Recently I had an opportunity to have lunch with Lamar Best, a retired general. He shared conversations he had with military troops in the mess hall. One of his favorite questions to ask was "Why are you a soldier?" Seldom did he hear "Because I want to have an opportunity to serve my country" or "I feel that freedom is worth defending." According to Dr. Best, the more common responses were along the lines of "Well, the judge said I had two choices: jail or the armed forces." Or "I had to pay my bills and couldn't find a job." When he mentioned this to the officers, they shrugged and said, "We work with what we're sent."

I wonder sometimes whether some laypeople feel like the officers. Certainly no pastor will be as crass as to say "It sure beats finding a real job." But the lack of work ethic among a few in the ministry implies the same. Why should being at work by 8:00 in the morning and being accountable at the office for one's hours during the day even need to be questioned?

A number of patterns of pastoral behavior are likely to make any church doubt a pastor's calling to local church leadership:

♦ Perpetual whining about how difficult the ministry is.

♦ Word on the street verifies they are campaigning for the next denominational post.

♦ A spouse who perpetually looks and acts like a first century martyr.

♦ A lifestyle of creative searching for handouts that puts a professional con-man to shame.

♦ Making no secret of a desire to teach some day in a college or seminary.

♦ The pastor's outside ministries no longer augment the purposes of the church nor provide significant benefit to the church; they rather give the appearance of holding a higher priority than the church.

While Candidating

Every senior pastor who experiences a candidating process will be asked three questions at some point. Number one: "What is the role of the pastor's wife?" Dr. Howard Hendricks gave us an amusing answer to this question when we were in seminary. "The role of the pastor's wife is to seduce the pastor!" Number two: "If you come here, what goals do you have for our church?" The best answer is obvious. "I don't know. But once I have arrived and have an opportunity to get better acquainted with the people, history, and environment, we will call together a group of leaders and decide this together." Number three: "Do you think God has called you to this church?" Unless you feel you have received a divine revelation regarding the specific location of service, a reasonable response is "I don't think God cares as much about where I am as He does about who I am [character] and what I am doing [convictions]. This assures our people from first contact that character and conviction issues are established and nonnegotiable. That is what leaders must bring to the table. If they don't share the convictions, they must look elsewhere for leadership. If they call you, they are buying into the convictions you bring.

The second thing the leader brings to the table is commitment. In this discussion the commitment relates to local church ministry. Turnaround churches *must* be led by a person who is committed to the local church. One of the big problems our churches have today is that they are too often led by people with a parachurch mindset. Parachurch leaders should lead parachurch organizations. Occasionally effective crossover takes place, but not often. These are two interrelated but distinct types of ministry. For effective leadership, turnaround churches need leaders committed to local churches.

Upon Arrival

Once you accept a call or appointment to a local church, you begin the task of convincing the layleadership, and then the entire congregation, that you are committed to *this* place of service. Some members will assume their church is a stepping-stone, especially if the church is larger than the one you left. They will also tend to think the worst regarding your motives if:

♦ they favored a rival candidate for the position, especially a relative, close friend, or existing staff member.

♦ they do not particularly like the search committee or district executive responsible for your placement.

♦ they have received inaccurate information regarding your last place of service.

♦ they were very fond of your predecessor. Note: When we arrived here in California in 1991, one woman who had been saved from a rough life-style under the loving leadership of my predecessor was so incensed by my arrival to replace the pastor she loved, that she threatened to have me taken out by a drive-by shooting. Welcome to California!

♦ you purchase a new home, significantly nicer than what they live in, or a new automobile, second home, or other status items. You may need to buy a home, but it may be wise to wait on other discretionary purchases.

Ways to Affirm Commitment to Your New Church:

1. Use the product you sell.

> You may not be overly enthusiastic about all the programs and ministries of the church when you arrive, however you must use them until they can be improved. People cannot sell a product they don't use. Can you imagine the CEO of Ford Motor Company driving into the lot one morning in a Chevrolet? If he were not lynched first, he would certainly be fired. But this logical principle of leadership seems to be lost on some would-be turnaround leaders. The organization in need of turnaround desperately needs a morale lift. If the one brought in to lead the turnaround, the one who has the single most power to bring about change and direction to the organization, does not use the products it is offering, how can anyone else believe in it?

What I do (or use) is the most powerful communicator of what I believe in! This extends to the leader's family and to all paid personnel. They simply must have enough faith in what the church will become and their ability to make it into what it needs to be—or others will continue to jump ship. This extends to all of the following:

- Children's programs

- Preschools and day schools

- Youth programs

- Athletic leagues and teams

- Music programs

- Training events

- Social functions

- Women's and men's Bible studies

I am not suggesting that the pastor or staff must attend every function. But especially in a turnaround situation, the leaders must convey the courage of a general in battle. If the plan is going to be successful, they must be willing to go with the troops. If the plan is doomed to failure, then let everyone out while it is still safe. If the leaders are confident of a brighter future, then they must demonstrate faith by personal utilization of the product they are attempting to sell others. Some will attempt to argue that the "product" is the gospel, not the programs. Ultimately, that is true. However, the gospel (and doctrine) comes under the heading of convictions, not commitment—of which we are speaking here. Not only must turnaround leaders be committed to the universal church (of which no one of us is the leader)—but to the local church, which they are called to and paid to lead.

2. Invest in the product you sell.

I am amazed at how many leaders of nonprofit organizations do not see the need to lead in personal giving. This can lead to a number of problems.

a. If the organization is a local church, such leaders are robbing God and thus have disqualified themselves from the right to lead.

b. Such leaders forfeit the respect of others who are supposed to follow them. Such information is usually supposed to be private, but eventually people find out. How can they respect a leader who is stingy, uncommitted, and, worst of all, hypocritical? Also, people in a nonprofit organization seem to know whether the commitment of their leaders is genuinely sacrificial or hypocritical. One tell-tale sign of leaders who are not leading in giving is their reluctance to talk about such matters.

c. Leaders who do not give sacrificially to an organization reek of a takers mentality. Soon much of their personal conversation is about "what is in it for me?" My perks, my salary, my travel, my benefits.

d. Such leaders do not grow faith muscles. Giving is first and foremost an act of obedience. Second, it is a process of faith-growth. God's laws of finances are designed to force us to live in the world of the unseen. Without faith it is impossible to please God, and so we end up leading work that is nonpleasing and unblessable by God. We wither away our days instead of participating in a perpetual endeavor of "body-building."

e. Such leaders have no personal stories and testimonies to give regarding the blessings of God's supernatural provision. People around them do not get to watch a life of faith in action.

f. Such leaders lose the realness of heaven. Where our treasure is, our heart will be also. If we are not laying up treasures in heaven where moth and rust cannot destroy and thieves cannot steal, then our conversation and focus will inevitably be earthbound. This provides no lofty goal worth significant sacrifice for our people.

g. When the manager of a mutual fund does not display confidence in the future of the fund, others will not invest heavily either. In fact, with all publicly traded stocks every officer of a corporation is required to report when they buy or sell. When all the officers are dumping their stock, it is often a dependable indicator to the small-fry investor that it is time to get out. Similarly, the pastor leaders of turnaround churches should indicate every way they can that they view the church as a solid buy.

If the primary manager of the stock does not have confidence, it makes good sense for the stockholders to call a meeting and find a new manager.

3. Defer gratification for the long-term good.

Sociologists teach that one of the characteristics of maturity is a willingness to defer gratification and work toward satisfying results over a long period of time. Turnaround leaders must convey early on to the team they are willing to postpone reward and personal benefits.

One of the surest ways to develop loyal team members and confidence in the leader is for the leader to communicate the following two commitments and back them up by action:

a. "We will sink or swim together. I will not benefit unless we all benefit. If we succeed, we do it together, and if we fail, we will do that together. But we are in the boat together."

Perhaps you recall the story of two guys fishing. One man looked toward the other end of the boat and saw to his dismay his fishing buddy carving a hole in the bottom. He yelled, "Hey, what are you doing?" His companion responded with disdain, "Mind your own business. I'm carving my end of the boat."

b. "We may need to make some sacrifices to turn this thing around. But if we do, all sacrifices will begin with me. I will not ask you to do anything that I am not personally prepared to do."

How many times have you observed the people at the top continuing to enjoy the good life while others are called upon to sacrifice? I have sat on boards where CEOs pass out substantial raises to themselves and their buddies while communicating that "times are tight and we're all going to have to do without." These messages kill whatever morale is left in the organization and create legitimate distrust. One safeguard is for leaders to maintain a consistent hands off policy in regard to their own financial package—unless it is to recommend necessary cuts.

Pastor Samuelson had served as senior minister at Way of Life Chapel for only two years. The summer after arriving, he discovered two financial realities. First, the church never met budget. In fact, those planning the budget did not intend for that to happen. The budget was viewed more as a nice intention and means of stretching the congregation. They also had a habit of dipping into designated funds to make payroll each summer with the hope that year-end giving and the emergency (though routine) curtailing of expenditures during the third quarter would permit them to complete each calendar year with some cash reserves on hand. After the second year of observing these patterns, Pastor Samuelson cautiously brought these matters to the governing board. They casually smiled, nodded, and said, "We know. That is just the way we've always operated."

Because of the growth during Pastor Samuelson's first two years, the Way of Life Chapel initiated a building expansion program. The three-year building campaign was modestly successful, but 150 people left. Things might have gone all right, except the area experienced a major recession. Housing prices dropped for the first time in memory and continued to do so for several years. Partially due to the recession and other factors, the major employer in town began lay-offs. Decreased housing values due to recession, unemployment, and lack of consumer confidence all combined to force some church members to make a choice between giving to the building program or to the general fund. Eventually all the cash reserves at Way of Life Chapel were depleted—before the predictably tough summer months. Pastor Samuelson knew he must lead to avert a crisis. He had confidence in the future of the chapel and truly believed that the building program was directed by the Lord and was the right and necessary thing to do. But gratification must wait.

Pastor Samuelson called the board together into his office for a stand up meeting. (This meant the meeting would only be for one item of business and it was not anticipated to be long.)

He began: "You know the financial history and practice of our church. You also have been involved in planning and leading our current building project. You are as aware as I am of the external issues impacting our area. Bottom line is that unless giving drastically increases or some changes are made, we will not be able to make payroll in one month. I do not anticipate a change in giving immediately, though I think we owe it to the congregation to let them know that if the giving patterns do not change immediately we will have no alternatives except to adjust major areas of expenditures.

"I have looked at our budget carefully. As you know, the church budget is approximately 40 percent for salaries, 20 percent for missions, and another 30 percent for nondiscretionary, matters such as mortgage, utilities, taxes, and so on. The remainder represents discretionary but critical programming.

"In order to make significant savings in expenditures, I see no choice but to cut all salaries, beginning with my own, and all missionary commitments by 5 percent until such times as this situation corrects itself. At the end of the year, if we have year-end giving to permit it, we can restore what is lost. I will also not recommend any salary increases until this financial challenge is resolved.

"Furthermore, I suggest we initiate a hiring freeze. When and if anyone—staff or missionary—resigns, we will not replace them until the giving has improved.

If these measures still do not accomplish what is needed, I have prepared a list of priority dismissals. Each staff position has been numbered in reverse order as to how their absence will adversely impact this church. We'll view it like peeling an onion. We will begin on the outside and work inward. Are there any questions or suggestions?"

The board members standing in the room looked at one another. Finally, one of them spoke for the group, "We'll be praying for you pastor." Another closed with prayer and the board went home.

Several things had occurred in that meeting. All of them were essential for the Way of Life Chapel to experience the 10 consecutive years of numerical and financial growth that followed:

a) Pastor Samuelson had communicated that he was committed to the church even if it meant some short-term personal sacrifice.

b) Pastor Samuelson had become the leader. The one who accepts responsibility for the finances of an organization is the leader of the organization. The board members were *not* unconcerned but relieved. They deal with financial realities all day in their place of work. They know what it is to make the hard and sometime unpleasant but necessary decisions. They were relieved that the burden for finances of the church would not be suddenly shifted to their shoulders. They now could go home and feel confident the church was in good hands.

c) The staff and missionaries would not be happy about the situation. But they could not say Pastor Samuelson was unfair or sheltering himself and his family from the call to sacrifice.

d) Pastor Samuelson communicated that he believed in the decision to build even if it meant some personal discomfort, and he planned to stay around to live with the decisions he had helped to make.

This is commitment!

When is it time to leave?

This is a frequently asked question. Of course there is a time for leadership to move on to other challenges. I have dealt with this at length in the Leading Turnaround Churches kit. It can be obtained through ChurchSmart Resources (1-800-253-4276).

4. Be committed to your philosophy.

Leaders will consult and work in partnership with the turnaround team in many areas. But they must bring convictions and philosophy to the table. A leader without an existing philosophy of ministry will confuse the team. One way to think of this is to picture the leader as a coach. Coaches at the little league level may or may not have a cogent management style, but by the time they make the major leagues the owners, players, and even the fans expect them to arrive at the ball park with a clear and consistent approach to the game. Changing approaches prevents putting together a team that can effectively implement the game plan. With a consistent coach, players understand what is expected of them and have the competency to play their role with excellence.

A number of ministry philosophies are available. Consult the materials of Willow Creek Association, Purpose Driven Church, or Growing Healthy Churches—to mention some of the better known. Or, perhaps, you can develop your own. In the appendix I'll share our home-grown philosophy. We call it Project PEDAR. Promotion; Evangelism, Discipleship, Assimilation, and Reproduction.

Whatever leaders bring to the church, they must be able to explain it and defend it, and be willing to live and die with it. Changing philosophies of ministries without rational and compelling reasons will diminish buy-in from the layleaders and set the work back years.

Coach/leaders need to bring a winning approach to the game of ministry. That is their responsibility.

CHAPTER 3

Courage

By Gene Wood

"Making people mad was part of being a leader.
As I had learned long ago . . .

an individual's hurt feelings run a distant second
to the good of the service."

—*Colin Powell*

Olan Harari, in his excellent book titled *The Leadership Secrets of Colin Powell*, comments:

Leadership can't be a popularity contest. Trying not to offend anyone or trying to get everyone to like you will set you on the road to mediocrity, because people who are afraid to make people angry are likely to waiver and procrastinate when it comes time to make tough choices. Leaders who care more about being liked than about being effective are unlikely to confront the people who need confronting . . . (p.18).

TRANSLATING TO BIBLE-SPEAK

Jesus told a parable about a man who was afraid to enter the investment/business market because of the fear of losing. You recall, of course, the Lord did not commend his timidity. Rather he stated that at the very least he could have drawn some minimum interest (low risk) and the insinuation, based upon the commendation of others who had a significant return on investment, is that He would have preferred the man took a higher degree of risk—even if it meant losing the capital.

Ministry is risky. Leadership is riskier. The first three dynamics reflect some degree of commitment. The last three are indicators of willingness to sacrifice for the cause, which is at the heart of courage.

These first three "Cs" are what the leader must bring to the turnaround situation. Bottom line: No effective team will be built unless they have a leader who consistently displays convictions, commitment, and courage. It may be difficult to find three words which better define the leadership which founded the church.

As tempting as it is to launch into a treatise on leadership in general, we want to focus on leadership as it relates to turnaround churches and team building.

WISE COURAGE

Since there will be no turnaround without bloodshed, the pastor must be wise in choosing where his blood is spilt. When doing turnaround seminars during the past two years, I've always returned to the premise that turnaround requires bloodshed. I was emphasizing this unpleasant reality at a seminar in Kentucky. During the break some of the participants told me how much they appreciated that reminder; then went on to tell me about a pastor in their fellowship who had been shot by a church bully, drug down the center aisle of the church, across the church lawn, across the street and left there bleeding.

For the record, when I speak of "blood shed," I am speaking figuratively. I sincerely hope physical violence of every sort can be avoided.

Nonetheless, effective turnaround leaders choose congregations where there is a calculated chance for turnaround (see *Leading Turnaround Churches* pp. 97-103). I would also encourage all bishops, overseers, denominational executives, and others who are in positions of "placing" or "appointing" pastors to a church to give even more attention to the matter of "readiness" of a church for revitalization and the "relatedness" of a church to its community. There are some great tools on the market today for assessing the likelihood of a church for change and vitality. I especially recommend the FRESH START tools written by Robert Humphrey (800-253-4276) www.startingfresh.org.

Let me reiterate what I stated in *Leading Turnaround Churches:* When a pastor-leader fails to ask the discerning questions prior to arriving on the scene and completely misses glaring roadblocks to growth, he logically forfeits a certain amount of respect from his most astute lay-leaders.

But once a decision is made to accept a call to a church, it is no time to question the marriage. From that point on, the pastor must lead with confidence of the calling. No whining allowed.

PROMISING PROTECTION

We'll talk in a later chapter about selection of staff. But upon arrival, the pastor must make one thing clear. The team in existence must be assured that if they do what they are asked to do, they will be safe. However, like any promise, this must be done with care and thought.

I am assuming the pastor is granted freedom to build a staff (volunteer and paid) which supplements his strengths and weaknesses (see appendix C), and this is definitely worth talking about long before agreeing to accept the responsibility of leading. The shepherd does lead the flock, not vice versa.

I recently received a "job description" from a sister congregation. The role was a significant executive level ministry position. The position had obviously been well thought out. But then I came to the section titled "Responsible To." It read:

> "They shall be accountable to and work under the church board or the Christian Education Committee appointed by the board."

I tossed the paper in the wastebasket. There is no one I dislike enough to send them into such an unworkable situation. As painful as this discussion is, it simply must be worked out prior to the arrival of a new pastor. Until churches allow the senior pastor to lead, we will probably continue to see one of two things: churches remain small enough that the staff issue never surfaces; or large churches with multiple staff will continue to be dysfunctional.

A rule of management states, "With responsibility must go corresponding authority." How can a board hold the pastor accountable for the work and decisions of the staff unless he has ultimate authority to remove, replace, and reward the staff appropriately?

Assume that this issue has been settled. Then the pastor can assure each staff member that if they do what they are asked to do, they will be secure. But they must understand being "okay" can include many things:

a. In time, their gifts and abilities will require they move to a different role.

b. In time, they may need to transition to some other location. But you will help them find a place more suitable for them.

c. They may be in the perfect place and can continue there as long as you are there.

But if they will be loyal and do what you ask of them— if they get fired, you'll both get fired. Such commitment and courage (i.e., confidence) will be refreshing to the staff you want to keep. At least they are clear on who they report to and the rules of engagement.

COURAGE TO REWARD THE PERFORMERS

Professional Staff

I once again refer you to the words of Harari: "Your best people are those who support your agenda and who deliver the goods. Those people expect more and deserve more, whether those rewards take the form of additional compensation, accolades, career advancement, assignments to plum . . . If they don't get what they expect and deserve, they become deflated, demotivated and cynical. Because they are marketable, they're the first ones to update their resumes" (p. 25).

Here is the problem in most churches:

"In most cases . . . we simply award across the board increases, percentage bonuses, or the like." Harari believes "this is just a leadership cop-out."

"That is why CEO's like Jack Welch, Sun Microsystems, Scott McNealy and Microsoft's Steve Ballmer are unapologetic about three things:

1. Providing everyone with resources and opportunity

2. Clearly providing the best players with the greatest rewards

3. Ensuring that chronic poor performers are shown the door

I am not suggesting a turnaround leader needs to fire all the staff who cannot perform with equal degrees of excellence. There must be some differences between business, in which the bottom line is profit, and the church where the bottom line is serving the Lord to the fullest considering each person's spiritual gifts (which the Holy Spirit gives), ultimate abilities (which we at least partially inherit) and opportunities. While the leader must consider the health and vitality of the church and at the same time expect hard work, loyalty, and commitment to the doctrines, philosophy, direction, and values of the church, it is unreasonable to think all staff members will achieve equal levels of competency.

Assume the staff member in question shares the doctrine, values, direction, and philosophy of the church and gives 90 percent effort. Assume he is loyal, but simply cannot fill the role necessary to help move the church where it needs to go. Too many leaders continue to give the same cost of living raises that all others receive, the same standardized perks and benefits, and even promotion due to tenure. In such cases the pastor is either incompetent or driven by fear. Fear of what the under-performing staff member will think/feel or fearful of the reaction from others in the church if their favorite staff member is somehow slighted. So what happens?

The over performers and exceptional hard workers on the staff soon understand their efforts to go the extra mile are not valued. The under performing staff discover they will be rewarded regardless of results. So one could expect the following:

- The best staff members sense that their extra efforts, unusual abilities, education, and skills are not valued, so they seek another place to serve—and easily find one.

- The less capable or less diligent staff discover that results do not really matter. They understand that what truly matters is getting rewarded and doing little is rewarded the same as doing much. So they settle comfortably into their status quo.

- In fact, staff members begin to understand the pastor-leader is fearful of public reaction regarding rewards. Therefore, it is better for them to invest time in making friends who will become their advocates rather than focusing on ministry. Thus a game of blackmail has begun.

Volunteer staff

The same issues of courage apply with volunteer staff. Only the Lord knows how many churches are held hostage by a musician, teacher, board member, or helpful custodian. But there are too many.

We are talking about courage to develop a turnaround team. This, by definition, assumes the church in question has experienced plateau or decline. When a pastor comes to give new leadership, he will inherit the existing lay-leadership.

If I have been in a leadership position (implying that I've helped make all the key decisions) for the past 20 years and the church is declining, *who* is responsible for the decline? Why would the church experience different results under my continued leadership? Some lay leaders need to apply the mirror-window principle. When things go wrong—look in the mirror.

If someone has been teaching a Sunday school class for 15 years and it has gone from 40 to 14, what logic drives such a teacher to believe he has the "gift of teaching"? When the Lord gives the gift of teaching, He gives others in the body the gift of listening.

If someone has been singing solos for 40 years, or playing the piano, or organ, or leading songs for the same period of time in the same church— and if everyone in the congregation can predict with pin point accuracy the ritual, style, and content of what they do—just maybe it's time to pass the baton, especially if the body is in perpetual decline. Obviously, what-ever is happening there is not appealing to anyone except the encrusted remnant.

If a man has been "ushering" for 30 years but does so by standing in the back talking with his friends, making a scene when he finally does enter the sanctuary, and has poor people skills—he is not helping the church.

Every pastor faces the unpleasant task of removing the entrenched team to make room for the new turnaround team. But it must be done. It can be done kindly, patiently, lovingly, and graciously. Of course, the dignity of these volunteers must be preserved if at all possible.

How might this change be made?

- ◆ If they offer to step down, accept their offer. One pastor in Texas told me that a particular man in the church had been the volunteer "custodian" of the church for decades. That meant he had all the keys to the church. When the pastor arrived for his first Sunday, the man humbly came to him and said, "Pastor, I've been doing this work of opening, closing, and caring for the property for a long time. Maybe now it's time for me to turn over the keys to you so you can find a younger person to do this." The pastor innocently said, "Okay" and reached out his hand and took the keys. Only later did he learn that this man had made the same speech to five other predecessors and each of them had made the mistake of saying, "Oh please don't do that, we need you." When in fact the keys had been a tool in the man's hands to give him authority far beyond what anyone could imagine.

♦ If the long tenured volunteer (a) has a good attitude and is cooperative (b) may be doing what they are doing simply because they honestly don't think there is anyone else who can and will, you could suggest they consider "mentoring" someone who you think might be able to grow into this ministry.

♦ Seize the opportunities to put a person of choosing in the role when they are sick or on vacation. Do not permit them to appoint their own replacement because they will likely choose someone more incompetent than they are. Their insecurity demands such a selection so they will be welcomed upon return.

♦ Be kind, but do not continue giving insincere compliments. If they ask how you feel about their ministry, be honest. Also be prepared to offer another place of ministry which may be more in keeping with their abilities and giftedness.

♦ When something absolutely unacceptable occurs, it may be time to confront the situation openly and ask them to step aside. When you do, tell them why it is time to make a change.

The last three recommendations all take courage.

COURAGE AND MONEY

A congregation must know that the budget approved will be managed well. They should not have to worry about the funds of the church. A common sense approach is to state, "We will not spend money here which we do not have. We are not the federal government and cannot print money." Say it; then do it.

Two assurances. Both require courage. One, we never overspend the budget allotments approved. This means we must plan well when the budget is presented. Two, we will not even spend the budget (including salaries and missions) if the funds are not coming in to support it.

This matter of fact commitment sends many messages. One is that you are confident in the future of this church and of your calling, therefore you are confident money will not limit what God intends to do here. When the leader is courageous enough to express this confidence, his convictions and commitment become contagious.

COURAGE TO STAY ON COURSE

It seems that one of the marked differences between pastors who develop turnaround teams and those who never do is found in the courage of turnaround leaders to set the course and not be deterred.

Few things are more disheartening to followers than to know their leader will likely reverse course based upon the last conversation he had. I have heard the staff of a large international organization admit they knew this was true of their CEO. He could sit and look you in the eye and say with seeming conviction "Yes, this is where we'll go." But you would wait for a week or a month, or six months, fully expecting a change of course that never came. The tragic thing is that the staff was always hesitant to pour too much time and energy in pursuing a directive because the work might very well be meaningless. Worse yet, they might destroy their own credibility by selling the "vision du jour" only to say "never mind" to those who worked for them.

Once the pastor has clearly defined convictions, absolute commitment to this place for this time, there must also be courage.

Will everyone be happy with the decisions made by the team? No! Will some leave? Possibly. Probably. But we're talking about churches in plateau and decline — seventy to eighty-five percent of all Protestant churches in the United States. The problem is epidemic. What has been done has been proven in-effective. In the coming chapters we will go into more detail on how the team helps develop the plans, programs, and direction of the local church. But make no mistake about it, the ability of the team to implement the plans will ride on the shoulders of the pastor's courage to keep them moving in the direction which is agreed upon. Here is where most pastors fail. They are good at writing purpose statements, values, mission statements, and even developing a strategy, philosophy, and goals for the church. They print them on expensive five color documents and pass them out. But little, if anything, gets done.

Change will bring opposition. Leadership cannot be a popularity contest. If a pastor desires to be liked more than he longs to see the local church move on to effective outreach and development of God's children, he simply will not be able to withstand the assault which comes with a turnaround. His motives will be questioned. His process will be questioned. His love for God will be questioned. His family may be attacked. But if he is confident that the right thing is being done, the leader must not altar the battle plan unless there are new and convincing facts to suggest he do so.

We'll deal later with how to arrive at the team-direction, but the team will never form a potent coalition for change until they are certain their leader will be there to see it through to successful completion. Courageous turnaround leaders share the common dynamic of deep and non-negotiable convictions along with a certainty of their calling to the church where they serve. They are God's leader for this time. They have a message which the community needs. They are convinced the present state of affairs in the church is unacceptable. They have worked through a planning process which is credible. All the data necessary has been gathered (when you have 70% of the information, move ahead with your gut intuition—we never have 100%).

Conviction:	Deals with the message!
Commitment:	Deals with the place!
Courage:	Reveals the confidence of calling!

Courageous leaders are confident. Once the above dynamics are assured, they believe with all their being they can change their environment. People who don't believe they can change their current reality will be pessimistic. Pessimism inspires no one. Optimism is the attitude that we are doing the right things, we are the right people, and we are in the right place. Now let's make a difference in our world. This attitude is contagious.

As I write this, I am on a plane making my way to Hong Kong and later into China. I'm excited because we have been working for years on a project to work alongside the Church in China and assist them in making

Bibles more readily available to the poorest rural people. It is May of 2003, and you may recall the SARS virus. Whether it turns out to be an epidemic of historic proportions or a scare is yet to be determined. What I do know is that as of today there have only been 250 people documented to have died from SARS in the world. By comparison 36,000 people per year die annually in the United States alone from the flu. Meanwhile entire economies are being disrupted, entire school systems are closed. People are afraid to travel throughout Asia and billions of people are living in fear. Primarily fear of the unknown. Fear is irrational. The result of fear is always larger than the reality which drives it.

On the other hand, the power of confidence and optimism are equally powerful tools for the good of a church. A pastor's perpetual optimism when combined with the other principles spoken of in this book will fuel success. Optimism is an expression of felt control. It destroys passivity and gives hope. Does this necessarily guarantee our plans will all work out? Of course not! But if our people lose heart, they will not be there to help implement the plans and nothing good will happen.

What if you fail? Winston Churchill is quoted as having said, "Success is measured by your ability to maintain enthusiasm between failures." In that sense a pastor's optimism and confidence will produce ultimate success.

The recent tragedy of the Columbia Space Shuttle (February 1, 2003) reminds us of the courage of our astronauts. I understand that as the space shuttle lifts off and moves through the pull of gravity, it begins to vibrate violently. Astronauts report it takes everything within them to not abort the mission. Then it moves into space and the shaking stops and then everything is almost eerily quiet. In order to avoid their natural instincts, they must have confidence in the engineers, contractors, and thousands of others who worked on their ship.

Don't abort the mission, pastor, once you have launched.

CHAPTER 4

The Engine of Turnaround: Convictions, Commitment, and Courage

By Daniel Harkavy

As I read the first three chapters, the word *heart* rang in my ears. Turnaround is all about heart. Any leaders who are brave enough to take leadership positions or recommit to leading churches that are in plateau or decline will need to have all of their heart in it. Heart is the most essential characteristic of successful leadership. You can possess all the leadership skills in the world, but you will fail to build a solid turnaround team if you lack heart! The local church will not succeed if led by a half-hearted leader.

Here is what I believe: the topics of the first three chapters of this book really constitute the engine of turnaround. I believe that you can be lacking in any of the topics covered in the following chapters and still enjoy a certain degree of success in leading a turnaround team. But if you are missing convictions, commitment, or courage, long-term success is impossible.

The beginning of chapter one stated there are volumes of books written on vision, mission, and purpose. As a coach, I have observed that only a small percentage of leaders who have read up on these topics have followed through and taken the time to really work through the process of creating their own vision. If you are one of the few who has done this, kudos to you. An even smaller percentage actually review their vision on a regular basis and use it for strategic planning, decision making, and team building. However, for your efforts to be truly effective, your vision must embody your convictions and commitment and feed your courage.

We at Building Champions are quite straight forward, and everything we create is very functional and relatively pain-free to implement. We designed a process to help business leaders clarify and articulate their vision. This very easy process worked so well with our executive clients that we modified it slightly and began using it a few years ago in our pastoral coaching organization—Ministry Coaching International.

This chapter will walk you through the specific action plans that will assist you with gauging where your heart is. It will then give you clarity on your vision and convictions, which will significantly affect your level of commitment and courage. Coaching is all about action plans. Every coaching session we have with our clients ends with an agreement between the coach and the client on what actions will be completed and when they will be done. I will do my best to coach you through each component of Leading Turnaround Teams so that you have clarity on how to implement the action plans that will take your leadership and team-building skills to new levels.

Creating Your Ministry Vision Document

ACTION PLAN:

Create or revise your vision document by following the Ministry Coaching International process.

Step One: Pray on your own and build a team of prayer warriors. You are after the vision God has in store for you as the leader of his bride. Without prayer, your vision is just that, *your* vision. This vision document will become the main tool used in building your turnaround team.

Step Two: Choose a date within the next 30 days to commit to writing or revising your vision. We suggest you block out 6 to 8 hours for this process. This should be viewed as the most important appointment you have all month. Think of it as your appointment with your Creator. You cannot pull a no-show. If you cannot make it, it must be rescheduled to another date. Only one reschedule is allowed.

Step Three: Leverage yourself by sharing what you're up to with your inner circle. This is the group that you're closest to and wants to see you succeed. Let them know what you're doing and when you're doing it, and ask them to hold you to it. Accountability for this type of work can do wonders for you, especially if you struggle with implementation.

Step Four: Choose a location that is conducive to creating—not your office or your home unless you have a spot that works for this type of work. We suggest a park, the beach, or a river, weather permitting. If weather does not permit, a lodge, library, or hotel room is acceptable. You must be alone and free from cell phones, e-mail, pagers, and team members. Our clients who have gleaned the most from this process are those who find a location that really allows them to connect with God.

Step Five: Bring your essentials: Bible, journal, and so on. *I know, you are pastors. You know the drill.*

Creating Your Ministry Vision

The way we have designed the tool was inspired by a great article in *The Harvard Business Review* by best-selling authors James Collins and Jerry Porras, who wrote *Built to Last* and *Good to Great*.

We have broken this exercise into the following four steps:

1. Convictions

2. Purpose

3. God-Sized Goals

4. The Future

1. Convictions

The first step is clarifying your convictions. I know that some of you have gone through this type of process and are crystal clear on your convictions. This exercise is for those of you who are now questioning the clarity of your own leadership core: are you leading by values or by convictions. In the business world, we establish our values based on our life experiences, beliefs, skills, opportunities, surroundings and education. Our convictions on the other hand, come from our heart and are the non-negotiables in our life.

Your role as pastor is more than a vocation. It is a calling from God himself. This calling comes with several built-in attributes, convictions being one of them. Some of them are identifiable the moment you receive clarity on your calling. For most of us, our convictions deepen and grow as we spend more time understanding who we have been created to be. They grow as we better understand whose image we have been created in and how God has called us to live. They grow and deepen as our perspective on life shifts from the temporal to the eternal.

Just last week, Building Champions hosted a marriage retreat for our team. We used a process created by Church Resource Ministries that requires you to look at the timeline of your life. You look at your past victories and challenges to gain more clarity on the defining moments of your life. This process enables you to see with more clarity who God has made you to be and what he has been preparing you for. It is powerful.

Many of my convictions have come from the painful seasons of my life. Here is an example. In 1998, I walked side by side with a very dear friend who was battling cancer. As a new believer, he was filled with questions about heaven and God's plan. We spent hours studying Revelation and talking about what heaven would be like and what role we would play in this next chapter of life. He transitioned from this life to the eternal life in less than a year at the very young age of 38, leaving behind a wonderfully sweet wife and a five-year-old daughter. I had the privilege of sitting by his side with his wife, mother, and sister as he took his last breath here on earth.

Before he passed, he had asked if I would speak at his funeral. He wanted to make sure that all of his friends and family members knew how to spend eternity with him. This was a life-changing experience for me. I cannot tell you how much I mourned this loss. I experienced huge pain, but God really spoke to me through these events.

One conviction that was developed as a result of this lesson was that *life is a vapor*. I had read that several times over the years but never really owned it. Another conviction is from the Psalms, *"So teach us to number our days so that we might gain a heart of wisdom."* Today I have deep convictions about the brevity of life and how I must order my days so that I am truly living a life that makes an eternal difference. I want to be a destiny changer and have a heightened sense of urgency to share the awesome news of God's redemptive plan with as many people as I possibly can. These are more than values in my life, they are convictions. I must fight to keep my time, talents, and treasures focused on the people and opportunities that will make an eternal difference.

The following process will assist you with clearly identifying some of your more significant convictions, those that will affect how you live and how you lead your team or the congregation God has called you to.

ACTION PLAN

Journal the following:

1. Review your past. How have life's peaks and valleys affected you? Just brainstorm and write down every celebration and every hurt. Who influenced you for the good? For the bad? What life events have made you who you are?

2. Review all that you have written out and identify what life lessons you learned from these seasons in life. Did you make any commitments or vows during these seasons of life? If so, what were they? Did certain verses or books in the Bible really speak to you? If so, what were they?

3. Write out the topics that cause you to rage or argue vehemently or speak about and study with unbridled passion.

4. What topics do you love to teach and are asked to present on a regular basis?

5. What would cause you to do the following:

   - Ask an elder to step down?

   - Ask a member to leave?

   - Devote large sums of church money?

   - Plead with the body?

   - Resign?

   - Risk getting fired for?

   - Fight with all force?

Write it all down. This thought process will bring your convictions to clarity. Now compile the list of convictions that make you who you are. Some of you will have a list of three to five, and some may have a list of ten.

Remember, your convictions:

- are intrinsic.

- define what you believe at the very core of your being.

- very rarely change.

- cause passion in you.

- will travel with you if you are called to another church or organization.

- will be valid and viable 100 years from now.

Here are some examples of convictions we have seen at Ministry Coaching International from our pastoral clients.

- Jesus Christ is true God and the only Lord and Savior.

- It takes faith to receive his spiritual blessings and enjoy his day-to-day care.

- There is nothing more important than growing close to Jesus and living for him.

- The Bible is inerrant and relevant in all times.

- Everyone needs Jesus; his followers need to share him with others.

- Holiness: We must have clean hands, a clean heart, and clean motives before God.

- Partnership: Build relationships: Partner with winners.

- Empowerment: Empower people to reach nations.

- Respect: Respect for the ministry of the Holy Spirit.

These convictions must be checked and, if godly, used to assist you with the many different decisions of your day. They make you the leader God has called you to be. There is one thing we can guarantee as we go through this process: God's grace is what bridges the gap between who we are and who he has called us to be.

2. Purpose

The second step of creating your ministry vision is clarifying your purpose. *What is this church about? What happens here? What is our mission?* As was stated in *Leading Turnaround Churches*, "Your purpose is the main thing." I will address this purpose-clarifying step by sharing the perspective of the church member.

"I belong to a mid-sized, nondenominational Christian church here in Lake Oswego. I serve as an elder on our leadership team. Our pastor, Guy Gray, has done a wonderful job of clearly communicating what our church, River West, is all about. Our purpose is "To build a community of Christ for the world." Guy has broken this down into four components: They are relevant teaching, meaningful worship, quality relationships, and compassionate outreach. These are the convictions he brings to us, the body of River West. Guy weaves the purpose and the convictions into our Sunday lessons and into every leadership meeting."

My family and I attended Grace Church of Glendora in the early 90s. This is how the church stated its purpose: "We exist to glorify God by developing committed followers to Jesus Christ who attract others to Him." The pastor, Gene Wood, wove our purpose into every meeting and incorporated it into just about every sermon. As a member, I was blessed by this because Gene and others in the church lived this purpose out. These years at Grace were my first years, my foundational years as a new believer. God used Gene and the body of Grace to help me develop into who God has called me to be.

The purpose of the local church in America means many different things to many different people. The constant, however, is that the church is in the business of populating heaven. The church is all about fulfilling the Great Commission and developing followers of Christ. At Ministry Coaching International, we coach pastors daily through this process of identifying themselves. Do not simply borrow the tag line from a megachurch that you read about. Ask God to reveal his purpose for you as the leader of the special church that He has called you to lead.

This purpose must totally capture the souls and hearts of your ministry team. Here are a few examples of purpose from some of our pastoral clients:

- The purpose of St. Paul is to recruit and grow faithful followers of Jesus who will find joy in serving him now and for eternity.

- We purpose to transform nations with the gospel of Jesus Christ by equipping and deploying high-quality missionary teams in partnership with leading indigenous ministries in target nations.

- To know Christ and to make Christ known

ACTION PLAN

Journal the following:

- ◆ Ask why? Start with a descriptive statement: "We exist to _____" Then ask, "Why is this important?" After a few whys, you will find that you're getting down to the fundamental purpose of your ministry calling.

- ◆ Is your statement short and concise? Jesus shared his purpose statement in John 10:10: "My purpose is to give life in all its fullness" (LIV). His purpose statement is short and concise and communicates the core purpose of his ministry.

- ◆ Does your statement communicate clearly the purpose and reason for being?

When you have articulated your purpose statement, you're half-way home! The convictions will become the filter for your decisions, and the purpose will guide your plans and ministry objectives. Your team will need to own them in order to lock on to the direction you have set for them. Remember, in leading turnaround, you cannot ask the body to follow along if all the leaders are not turning around together.

3. God-Sized Goals

In their article "Building Your Company's Vision," Collins and Porras use the term *Big Hairy Audacious Goals*, or BHAG. This sounds huge, doesn't it? But I think God-Sized Goals are even bigger. Your goals should be so big that God *must* intervene if they are to be realized. They cannot be reached by human effort alone; they are supernatural.

The third step in creating your ministry vision is articulating these God-Sized Goals. What is it that you envision? Can you see having a team of disciple-making lay leaders mentoring 50 percent of your members? How about having several community centers being led by your incredibly gifted staff of associate pastors? Maybe it is having 80 percent of your members fully engaged in Christ-centered community groups. Is it having your own sanctuary with ample parking and classrooms and room for effective neighborhood outreach? Or, maybe it is a certain number of baptisms per year. I know this—God is at work and he loves to blow us away with his gifts. At Ministry Coaching International we have had the opportunity to speak with many of this generation's most gifted and blessed church leaders; the stories we hear confirm that God's heart is for his bride, the church.

Here are a few examples of God-Sized Goals from our pastoral clients.

- Become the leading supplier of high-impact Christian missionaries and programs to the church in the developing world.

- Equip quality missionary candidates with theological, spiritual, and communication skills and place them with high-achievement partners in developing nations.

- Calling people to be transformed by the power of the Holy Spirit and to transform their world.

- Our goal is to be the largest, steadily growing, vibrant, biblically sound, spiritually alive gathering of disciples in the Eastern District.

ACTION PLAN

Journal the following:

- What do I see God calling us to accomplish?

- Is it so exciting in its own right that it will continue to keep the leadership team motivated even if I am called away or taken home?

- Is it clear and compelling?

- Does it serve as a unifying focal point of effort?

- Does it act as a catalyst for team spirit?

- Does it have a clear finish line so that my team will know when we achieve it?

- Is it tangible, energizing, and highly focused?

4. The Future

The fourth step in creating your ministry vision is my favorite part of this process: articulating the future. This is where the picture changes from black-and-white to color. As you may know, most team members in the business world did not join teams because of pay or benefits. They joined the team because of leadership and culture. In the church world we add *calling* to this equation. Over the years, we at Building Champions have coached hundreds of executives to improve their recruiting and team-building skills. Too many of them operate from the head and offer form and function, but they fail to connect with the hearts of potential and existing team members and consequently often wonder why they are not attracting and keeping top talent.

People follow leaders who are conviction driven and have the ability to paint a picture of the future. Superstar recruiters and team builders can paint this picture so that it includes every potential and existing team member. They can articulate what it will look like, feel like, and be like for each team member when they cross the finish line.

Here is an example of a future articulated by one of our pastor clients.

Community Impact:

> In ten years, St. Paul Lutheran Church will be a household name in Batavia, known for its members' deep commitment to living for Jesus by serving others and their passion for sharing the joy of faith in Jesus.

> The surrounding community will recognize that, at St. Paul, people will experience the presence and love of Jesus through the love of our people and the Spirit-filled worship and faithful teaching.

> Everyone who comes in contact with any of our ministries will clearly see that Jesus holds first place in all that we do, that His power is clearly at work here at St. Paul.

> Everyone who comes in contact with St. Paul will be drawn closer to Jesus and see what He can do as He transforms peoples' lives.

> Our worship and educational opportunities will be looked to as examples of doing it right, God's way, by other churches in western New York.

> The community will recognize our music and outreach events as top-notch events that even non-Christians won't want to miss.

St. Paul will be perceived as a church with no walls; our service and witness and love will be as apparent out in the community as on our campus.

Outreach:

St. Paul will be a missionary growing church, preparing and sending out children and adults into the community equipped to live for Jesus, love like Jesus, and call others to follow Jesus every day.

St. Paul will hold frequent seasonal outreach events targeting the unchurched community.

There will be intentional ongoing outreach to all visitors who come onto our campus.

Love and joy will be obvious not only when you step onto our campus but also when you meet our members off campus.

Visitors will come from all around to find out and experience for themselves how powerfully Jesus works in and through the lives of disciples who stay close to Him.

Our leaders and members will be so excited about our ministry that they will be constantly inviting friends and neighbors to come to St. Paul to see the joy and vitality of life in a healthy Christian congregation devoted member by member to serving Jesus.

People who want to get close to Jesus will be drawn to St. Paul.

People will be so drawn to Jesus here that every week new people will be coming to faith in Jesus.

St. Paul will be seen as a group of Christians who have learned to effectively communicate the Good News of Jesus to new generations, sharing this message with each generation in a way that will have the deepest impact for the hearer.

Spiritual Growth:

Over 75 percent of the membership of St. Paul will be participating in spiritual growth classes weekly.

Over 85 percent of the membership of St. Paul will be in worship weekly.

People who come to St. Paul enter a planned path for their step-by-step spiritual growth and discipling.

Personal ministry, member to member and member to non-member, will be evident everywhere you go.

This will be a church where God's Word is taught, loved, and lived.

St. Paul will be recognized for its first-rate biblical teaching and preaching.

The Spirit of God is evident, flowing through our members in worship and in service, when they gather on campus and when they disperse into the community.

The staff and leaders won't be able to imagine serving anywhere else but here, surrounded by Jesus' active blessing and guidance.

Service:

Over 50 percent of the membership of St. Paul will be actively serving or ministering according to their giftedness in the church or in the community.

When someone in the church or in the community is in need, St. Paul people will be the first ones to respond with help.

Members will be counseled into personal opportunities for ministry.

St. Paul will be an example of genuine Christianity put into practice daily by young and old alike.

"Management requires head knowledge; leadership requires heart passion."

ACTION PLAN

Journal the following:

- What will it be like once we accomplish the God-Sized Goals?

- Who will we become as we take this journey together?

- Where will we personally and organizationally grow?

- What will we be known for in the community?

- What will we offer?

- What will our leadership team look like and how will we function?

- What will my role be?

- How will we help other church leadership teams and congregations?

You want to be able to see it—to almost smell it and taste what it will be like after years of obedience and excitement as you take your team on this turnaround journey.

Are They Onboard?

It is now time to bring it all together. At Ministry Coaching International we have our clients collect the results of each of these four steps into a document under the heading "The Vision for Our Church." Once you complete this, it is time to begin sharing it with your leadership team. The process of creating and sharing your vision will bring clarity to you and to your team.

I suggest meeting with them one-on-one before bringing them all together to discuss it. Make sure you have a copy for every team member and then read it to them and have them offer input. This does not mean you need to adjust it as they direct; you are really looking for buy-in as you meet with them. Can they see where it is you're being led to take them? Does this stir them? Do they get excited about the role they are going to get to play?

This document is your road map. It is to be used on a daily basis. Read it aloud to your team every month. Every team member should keep a copy of it. All leaders must know the convictions and purpose well. Always refer to this vision document when faced with new opportunities and challenges.

Your convictions will regularly come under attack. Your purposes will frequently be questioned:

- *"Is this program really important?"*

- *"Why must we change how we conduct our services?"*

- *"Steve is so nice and has been here since the church started; you can't replace him!"*

- *"Stop this outreach! No way! Can we continue it?"*

- *"Um, I am sorry, Pastor; it does not look like we can pay our bills this month."*

Oh yes, you have and will hear it all. Will this rock you? Or will you go back to your convictions and your vision and pray to God to give you the courage to lead his bride back to vibrant health? That is what he has in store for you—vibrant, abundant, Spirit-filled health. He has called you to build up his church in such a way that the fruit is so plentiful that its aroma can be smelled and its beauty seen from miles away. When you and others read your vision, they should not only see it, but also be able to feel it. This is the first step to leading a turnaround team.

ACTION PLAN

Bring it all together in 30 days:

- Combine the results of each of the four steps in the vision-clarifying process into one document.

- Share it one-on-one with your closest leaders or advisors within the next 30 days.

- Make any necessary adjustments.

- Share it with the congregation.

- Print it and make copies available to everyone.

- Read it daily and pray through it to keep you on track.

- Share it with the team in your monthly staff and leadership meetings.

- Preach it.

- Use it for interviewing and hiring.

- Use it for performance reviews and terminations.

◆ Adjust it regularly as led by the Lord.

◆ Expect to see it fulfilled; God is about doing wonderful things!

More on Commitment

Creating your vision is one thing; living it is where the real work begins. In chapter two Gene shares many practical insights and strategies on how to lead with commitment. You have been challenged to lead with commitment in your work hours, giving, program support, church finances, philosophy, and team. This section brings some business insights to the topic of commitment, as well as giving you specific action plans. The purpose here is to increase your level of personal and team commitment.

Gene says 8:00 a.m. is to be your start time. He is being easy on you! I know that Gene is an early riser, as are most great leaders. I'm not saying that you're not a great leader if you sleep until 8:00. My observation is that most great leaders rise before or with the sun. Jesus himself woke up a long while before daylight and departed to a solitary place to pray. (Mark 10:45).

In the business world the leader is the pacer of the team. You can see how committed the leader is by looking at how committed his team is. This can be a very painful rule. If "Bringing glory to Christ by exemplifying excellence in how we lead and live" is a conviction of yours, then your day must reflect it. You set the pace, the hours, the intensity, and the feel. We have coached many leaders who are only working part-time, and just as many who are so driven and out of balance that they are working twice as much as they should.

Each of you has different life situations, different stories. There is no one perfect time-block model for all of you. I think one of Satan's biggest tactics is to use guilt to delude you, the pastor, into thinking you need to do it all on your own. Many of you have high D behavior patterns, which means that you are dominant and driven. It is easier for you to fall prey to this lie of Satan than for a leader who is a high I or S ("Influencing" and "Steady" in the DISC language). Satan has been very successful in deceiving many of your peers by getting them to lose sight of what God has called them to be as husbands and fathers. Many of them are burning out due to losing the discipline of observing the Sabbath. Some are having to leave their church or leave the ministry altogether.

One of my mentors, Dennis Blevins, has been discipling me for the last five years. He is a renaissance ministry man as he serves as an executive pastor, a disciple maker with the Navigators, a leader with T-Net, and a coach with Ministry Coaching International. He has really helped me understand the need for discipline in my walk with the Lord. I have learned that the more committed I am to my morning quiet time and my retreats with the Lord, the better my relationship is with him. The better my relationship is with him, the more committed I am to living according to his plans for my life. Satan wants us to think we don't have time for this. We are too busy; God will understand, and we will meet with him later. That is a lie!

We know the attack is much more intense for you as pastors. He wants you to think that your lesson preparation time will suffice. Not so. This is work, and, while you may be learning, often it is head work and not heart work. We have had several pastors report that their only God time is when they are preparing for next week's sermon. We have heard that there is no real intimacy with him and that many of you feel very distant from him. He wants more time with you—time to speak to you about who you are in him, and about what he wants to do in your life and about the lessons he has in store for you. This is relationship time that takes place when you intentionally meet with him for refueling and building the most crucial relationship in your life.

The foundation for the coaching model of Ministry Coaching International is the Core4©. It consists of four cornerstones of a person's vocation and life:

1. Life Plan

2. Ministry Vision

3. Ministry Plan

4. Priority Management

Using this model enables us as coaches to help our clients gain clarity on the cornerstones of their vocation and life. Once a client has articulated each of these cornerstones, we can coach them on any topic that is relevant to them.

Living a Deliberate Life, The Life Plan

The first cornerstone of the Core4 is the Life Plan. Determining your Life Plan entails identifying the most important aspects of your life, then creating the vision, purpose and action plans to increase your net worth in each "life account." With our business clients, we teach that real success in life means building net worth in all life accounts, not just financial and vocational. Having a Life Plan is an absolute must if you want to truly master priority management. Each of the four cornerstones integrate with each other. Life Planning is much more than goal setting: Goal setting is about reaching a final destination, but Life Planning is about making the right decisions daily so that your life is an abundant journey.

This is where your personal commitments can be identified. Quality team members don't want to follow leaders who are so out of balance that their pace and expectations will take them out of ministry over the long haul. They want to follow leaders who are living excellence inside and outside of the organization. Our motto is that we coach leaders so they can build businesses that enable them to be more purposeful in business and in life. We coach pastors so they can live lives that enable them to lead and build up churches that glorify God. Your life must reflect his plans, purpose, peace, joy, love, rest and abundance in order for the team to live it. Your team must live his plans, purpose, peace, joy, love, rest, and abundance in order for the church body to live it. Your church body must live it in order for the community to experience and want it.

So here is the question. Are you committed to building a team of leaders who will grow and thrive under your leadership? If so, you must demonstrate his presence in every aspect of your life. This means your marriage, family, health, purity, finances—everything. To whom much is given, much is expected. The Life Plan will help you set a healthy pace.

We have created a wonderful tool to help our pastoral clients develop their Life Plans. You can obtain a copy of it by going to our website at *www.ministrycoachinginternational.org*

ACTION PLAN

Complete or update your Life Plan

The plans of a man's heart are deep waters,
but a man of understanding draws them out.
Proverbs 20:5

Step One: Pray on your own and seek out a team of prayer warriors to pray for you. You are after God's plan for your life. Ask him to show you what he has in store for you in all areas of life.

Step Two: Choose a date within the next 30 days to commit to writing or revising your Life Plan. We suggest you block out eight hours for this process. This is to be viewed as the most important appointment you have all month! It will be with your Creator. You cannot pull a no-show. If you cannot make it, it must be rescheduled to another date. Only one reschedule is allowed.

Step Three: Choose a location that is conducive to creating—not your office or your home, unless you have a location that is secluded. Again, we suggest a park, the beach, or a river, weather permitting. If weather does not permit, use a lodge, library, or hotel room. You must be alone—no team members—and free from cell phones, e-mail and pagers. Our clients who have gleaned the most from this process are those who find a location that really allows them to connect with God.

Step Four: Leverage yourself by sharing what you're up to with your band of brothers or group of leaders—the group that you're closest to, who want to see you succeed. Let them know what you're doing and when you're doing it, and ask them to hold you to it. Accountability for this type of work can do wonders for you, especially if you struggle with implementation.

Step Five: Bring your essentials.

Commitment to Doing What You Do Best, The Ministry Plan

If you are following the road map, your Life Plan and Ministry Vision documents are done. The third cornerstone in our Core4© Model helps you to identify with what activities you need to be filling your calendar. We call this the Ministry Plan. What we have gleaned from coaching our executive and entrepreneurial clients is that the business plan must be easy to follow if it is to really influence your day-to-day decisions and behaviors. To be effective, the Ministry Plan must be a good and concise read. It should show you the following three things with absolute clarity:

1. Your desired end result. What is the team or church endeavoring to accomplish or measure?

2. Your daily disciplines. These are the three to six activities that you are absolutely the best at.

3. Your projects or enhancements. What will you work on this year to move you closer to making our vision a reality?

Step One: What is your desired end result? What are you as a team or church endeavoring to accomplish or measure? This is key to really leveraging your skills and building a turnaround team. What are you going to shoot for? Are you shooting to have 250 in Sunday morning services? Are you targeting 25 baptisms this year? Are you looking at increasing giving by 25 percent? What tangible objective are you reaching for this year?

ACTION PLAN

♦ Write out what specific objectives you have for the church this year. Many of our business clients will measure growth in gross revenue and improvements in net income. Some measure the number of people served or products manufactured. What is it for you and your church?

♦ Write it down on an annual, monthly, weekly, and daily basis.

Step Two: What should your daily disciplines be? These are the three to six activities that you are absolutely the best at—your high-payoff disciplines (HPOD's). How much time do you spend doing them on your normal day? We take our clients through a process to identify their HPOD's and LPOD's (low-payoff disciplines). By spending time focusing on your HPOD's, you add maximum value to your team and the church. They are the activities that allow you to fully utilize your gifts, and when doing them, you are energized. They are the activities that the church is really paying you for. LPOD's are the activities that others on your team could do. They do not challenge you or cause you to fully use your gifts. They could be done by a person who earns a lesser wage than you. As coaches we strive to help our clients fill their calendars with the HPOD's and to delegate, delay, or drop the LPOD's. The best way to identify your HPOD's and the amount of time you are allocating to them each day is to do what we call time track.

ACTION PLAN

What are my HPOD's?

1. Create a daily schedule in 15-minute increments starting when you begin your workday and ending when you stop. It will look something like this:

Day: Date:

Time	Activity
7:00-7:15	
7:15-7:30	
7:30-7:45	
7:45-8:00	
8:00-8:15	
8:15-8:30	
8:30-8:45	
8:45-9:00	
9:00-9:15	
9:15-9:30	
9:30-9:45	
9:45-10:00	
10:00-10:15	
10:15-10:30	
10:30-10:45	
10:45-11:00	
11:00-11:15	
11:15-11:30	
11:30-11:45	
11:45-12:00	
12:00-12:15	
12:15-12:30	
12:30-12:45	
12:45-1:00	
1:00-1:15	
1:15-1:30	
1:30-1:45	
1:45-2:00	
2:00-2:15	
2:15-2:30	
2:30-2:45	
2:45-3:00	
3:00-3:15	
3:15-3:30	
3:30-3:45	
3:45-4:00	
4:00-4:15	
4:15-4:30	
4:30-4:45	
4:45-5:00	
5:00-5:15	
5:15-5:30	
5:30-5:45	
5:45-6:00	

2. Make 5 copies of this so you can track your activities for an entire week. We call this time tracking.

3. Enter in everything you do every 15 minutes. Whom did you call, talk with or meet with, and why? What did you read or study? What did you write or e-mail? Write it all down. I know you may hate doing this, but please, trust me on this one. It is a huge eye-opener, for most, to go through this process and identify all of your daily actions that could be done by someone else or not done at all.

4. Highlight all HPOD's with a green marker and all LPOD's with a yellow marker. You may be challenged to identify which are which. In the business world, we ask the client to identify their desired hourly wage. If you make $40,000 per year, you earn about $20.00 per hour. We then ask, "What activities are you doing that you could pay another person $10.00 an hour for?" What you will realize is that you are stealing from the church when you're getting paid $20.00 per hour and doing minimum-wage work. Not only this, most of the time we also lose heart in our vocation when the majority of our time is being spent in the LPOD's; they drain us!

5. Total the amount of hours in a day that are spent in the HPOD's versus the LPOD's. How much more time would you have in your day, week month, and year to lead and grow if you could effectively delegate the activities that another person would be better skilled at doing? We have seen pastors gain 50 days per year by going through this process!

6. Solidify your HPOD's—the activities that energize you and cause you to fully use the gifts God has blessed you with. We call these your Zone activities. As I stated earlier, you should have three to six of them. Write them down and ask your spouse, your band of brothers, or your group of leaders for affirmation. Ask God to affirm these zone activities in you. At Building Champions, we call these the Disciplines of a Champion. You can get a great idea of what your week should be filled with by reading Chapter 6 of Gene's first book, *Leading Turnaround Churches*.

Step Three: What projects or enhancements will you work on this year to move you closer to making your vision a reality? This step is crucial if you want to improve how you and your team strategically operate. What three to five projects are most important this year? They could be to create a church member database and photo directory, create the new building fund-raising plan, add a second service, or add a full-time worship leader.

Many leaders struggle with bringing projects to completion because they do not take the time to identify what projects are most important and then to realistically prioritize what resources they have to accomplish the task. The result is starting and stopping on multiple projects without ever really bringing them to completion, or not starting any new projects at all because there is so much to do that you feel overwhelmed by the enormity of it all.

As the leader, it is your responsibility to make these decisions. Your team will have a much higher degree of confidence in you if you have the ability to pick and prioritize your projects with confidence. When they see this in you, they will commit to taking on what they need to do in order for the church to improve.

ACTION PLAN

Identify the Improvements

1. List out every improvement you want to make.

2. Identify the projects that will cause physical, financial, or spiritual pain if not dealt with this year. If there are none that fall into this category, move on to the next step.

3. Identify every improvement that will affect the spiritual growth of the body, attract more people, enhance the ministry experience, increase giving, cut expenses, or enable you or your leadership team to better function.

4. What resources are needed for each of them, for example, personnel, time, financial, team etc...?

5. When would you like to see each improvement completed?

6. Choose the top three to five. Can you and your team complete them in the next 12 months?

7. If not, schedule them for next year.

Congratulations! You have now completed your Ministry Plan. This is a document you will share with your team, review daily, and use for all decision making and scheduling. We will discuss this further in the next chapter.

A completed Ministry Plan will look something like this.

More on Courage

As Gene stated, "No effective team will be built unless they have a leader who consistently displays convictions, commitment, and courage." Coaching people through these first three C's has been the most difficult part for me. The action plans that I have given you, with prayer, will increase your levels of commitment and courage, giving you and your team clarity on your convictions.

When you have taken the time and given your all to the previously given action plans, your courage will increase. In Chapter Three Gene gives clear and specific action plans that when followed will demonstrate courage. I see courage as the outward manifestation of faith. David's courage in his battle against the Philistine giant was caused by his huge faith and understanding of the enormity of God. God loves his bride the church. His plan is for his bride to prosper and flourish. His plan is for you to lead with no fear.

I have four children. My oldest daughter, Allie, is 13, and my sons, Dylan and Wesley, are 11 and 8. My newest arrival, Emily, is two months old. My boys and I have created a special kind of salute that communicates the truths in 2 Timothy 1:7: "For God has not given us a spirit of fear, but of power, love and sound mind." We flex our right bicep, touch our chest over our heart, and then touch our head. With this we communicate that we are God's warriors. I love it! After I pray over them at night and tuck them in, and when they are leaving for the day with friends, we give each other the Hark-man salute.

I think 2 Timothy 1:7 is one of the best verses for Turnaround leaders to anchor in their heart. Satan tries to instill doubt and fear wherever he can.

He has been working my daughter Allie with some nighttime fears, and I have been doing some "sword" work with her. I have written out four verses on 3 x 5 cards for her to review before she goes to bed every night. I see Satan's plan at work in the life of the body at all ages. It starts when we are young, and his attack increases as we become more dangerous to him in our work for God's kingdom. Our instructions to combat the fear and increase the courage are straightforward: own God's words, live them in a very real way. Camp on them and really understand the power that comes from knowing and living his Word.

Pastors, God has not given you a spirit of fear; Satan has. As I stated earlier, leading a team, especially through turnaround, requires huge courage, the courage of William Wallace in *Braveheart*.

The next anchor verse for me with regard to courage is Exodus 15:3. I have read John Elderedge's *Wild at Heart*, *Sacred Romance* and *Waking the Dead*. I have also been to two of his Wild at Heart retreats. God has used him in a big way to communicate who Jesus is and who he has called men to be. This passage in Exodus states, "The Lord is a warrior; the Lord is his name." I don't know about you, but when I think warrior, I think courage. Here is the wonderful thing that John taught me at his retreat: God is a warrior and I am made in his image. Therefore, I am a warrior! How about you—do you see yourself as a warrior for his kingdom? You *must* be if you're leading his church from the pit of despair to the heights of his glory! Our church needs warrior leaders.

Listen to the mandate in 1 Corinthians 16:13-14: "Be on the alert, stand firm in the faith, act like men, be strong. Let all that you do be done in love." Don't you just hear it? Paul is saying, "Men be courageous! Have no fear, act like the men I have made you to be! Don't be weak or insecure, be brave and operate from your hearts, in love."

No matter what season your church is in, God's plan is to strengthen you and to uphold you. Isaiah 41:10 has spoken to me in big ways over the years:

"Do not fear, for I am with you;

Do not anxiously look about you, for I am your God.

I will strengthen you, surely I will help you,

Surely I will uphold you with my righteous right hand."

Your team needs this characteristic from you in the worst of ways. If they see that you're insecure, worried, bent towards anger, or isolated, they will see right through you. They will see the cowardly lion from *The Wizard of Oz* instead of the Savior Aslan from *The Lion, the Witch, and the Wardrobe*.

Here are some solid action plans to increase your courage.

ACTION PLAN

Increase Your Courage

- ◆ Make your morning time with him a nonnegotiable. Go to new depths with him in your quiet time. If it is stale at home, take a day and go for a hike or canoe ride with him. Take a walk on the beach with him. Turn over your fears and worries to him; his shoulders are so much bigger than yours. Ask him to give you what he has in store for you and to show you where you might be limiting him.

- ◆ Surround yourself with a few brothers. We are designed for fellowship. Prayerfully consider who God wants you to lock arms with. Meet with them regularly for time in the Word and, more important, time in each other's life. Don't stand out there alone; Satan's plan is to isolate you and pick you off. This strategy has proven to be hugely successful; just look at some of your peers.

- ◆ Read your Life Plan, Ministry Vision, and Ministry Plan no less than weekly.

- ◆ Read your Ministry Vision in your monthly meetings with your team.

- ◆ Don't make ministry decisions without measuring them up against your Ministry Vision and Ministry Plan documents.

- ◆ Read the first three chapters of this book no less than three times so you can really absorb all of the content Gene has shared.

Fire up the Turnaround engine and put the pedal to the metal!

CHAPTER 5

Competency

By Gene Wood

A church in serious need of turnaround is filled with pessimism, denial, complacency, nostalgia, entrenched dysfunctional behaviors, and unhealthy power issues. Overlaying it all is an attitude of hopelessness. The church members really believe they have probably done or are doing everything that can be done but God simply does not want to do any more among them than what they are currently experiencing.

Yet, they call you to lead them. During the courting (candidating/recruitment) process, words were probably spoken about what an exciting future the church could have. But, once you begin your work, the stark realities come to light.

I believe that many of the 320,000 plateaued and declining churches in our country have men, women, and young people who earnestly desire to see their church experience renewed vitality. They see what is happening in other places and want the same excitement, growth, and evidence of the Holy Spirit's working where they are. But they've become convinced that will not happen.

One reason, of course, for this thinking is the reality they live with year after year of declining numbers and few coming to faith in Christ, even fewer making public commitments regarding their faith, and still fewer joining the church and developing into productive reproducing members. If they are the leaders and are doing all they know how to do yet nothing is happening, their conclusion is that nothing can be done there. Or some rationalize that what is happening (plateau and decline) must be what God wants to occur in their church for sovereign reasons known only to him.

If Dale Carnegie taught us anything in his classic *How to Win Friends and Influence People*, it is that "people never admit they are wrong." So, in spite of the fact the Lord clearly declared, "I will build my church," and despite the fact we have more freedom, more money, more technology, and great openness to the gospel today—70-85 percent of all Protestant churches in our country wring their hands and say, "God may work, but there just isn't anything more we can do here that will make a difference in our community."

"But we must hire a pastor. That is what churches do. We need someone to preach a sermon on Sunday, visit the sick, perform the ordinances, counsel those irascible young people, and officiate at weddings and funerals. Sure it's expensive, but we'd really like to have someone here full-time as long as we can. Never know when we might need someone to open the church for us during the week." They are looking for a chaplain, a caregiver. Pastors often arrive viewing themselves as spiritual generals prepared to lead an assault on the gates of hell.

You may think the above description is harsh. But I think it far too often reflects the reality. Hundreds of pastors go each year into such a conflicted situation.

Your church's reality may or may not be this dire. Regardless, it does illustrate the need for the pastor to make the people believe he actually can lead them to a preferable tomorrow. Things do not need to continue in decline. The best days are yet ahead. God is still alive, and he is alive here, and he wants to build his church here! That must be communicated loudly and repeatedly and convincingly. Saying it is the easy part. Causing a declining congregation to actually believe it is what this chapter is all about.

Pastors create belief by establishing the competency of their own leadership. Church members must see alignment between what is said and what actually occurs.

Establishing Competency in the Beginning

I accepted a call to come to Grace Church of Glendora. Our first Sunday was to be the first week in January 1991. I realized that I was in many ways entering into a new world. This was California, not Ohio. This was a true metropolitan area. It doesn't get much bigger than L.A., in our country at least. My predecessor was an excellent preacher. The church was significantly larger than any I had served. I needed counsel.

I called Larry and asked if he would make time for me as we drove through Tempe. He had effectively led a church over the 800 barrier once and was now leading a congregation numbering in the thousands. I wanted advice from someone who had personal experience.

When we met for breakfast, he shared several helpful pieces of advice. The suggestion that proved most helpful was something I would never have considered. Larry said, "Gene, if you've got anything really good in your gun, fire it quick." I am not sure those were his precise words, but he was reminding me that we only have one opportunity to make a first impression: Make it a good one.

When I took law enforcement classes in junior college, a professor spent an entire class period stressing how critical the first 20-60 seconds are when an officer stops someone and walks up to their car window. Those seconds largely determine the tone for the rest of the encounter. In those seconds, the driver is assessing whether he or she likes the officer, can trust the officer, and will cooperate.

If you have any good sermons that will define your ministry, passions, and hopes for the church, use them. If you have any good ideas that are sure-fire wins, use them.

That was good advice, and it still holds. Yes, it will take years before most congregations truly look to the pastor as a trusted leader. Trust is earned. But one way to begin earning it from the beginning is to find some things that have a risk-reward ratio in your favor.

In our first couple of Sundays at Glendora, I preached what I called three "main-thing" messages. They simply reminded our people of the task of the church. Point one: Jesus came to seek and to save those who are lost. Point two: Jesus said "As the Father sent me, now I'm sending you." Point three: What are we going to do about this?

Not profound. But it did represent my heart and what I hoped for our church. I have begun every year since with a main thing message.

I honestly can no longer recall many of the specific steps I took. However, the call to me as pastor centered on two major commitments:

a commitment to lead and a commitment to see our church become outward focused. Based on those commitments, here are some of the major actions I took.

- Began a training program and implemented weekly evangelism and outreach efforts.

- Sat with each staff member to hear what they thought their job was; then articulated what I thought it was going to be.

- Began to take direct oversight of the staff and lead staff meetings (a departure from what had been done).

- Began to act as chair of the elder board. The by-laws stated that the senior pastor was the presiding elder, but my predecessor had somewhat delegated that to a lay elder.

- Made it clear that I would be working closely with the elected leadership of our church. Apart from that there would be no "special" people—or to state it in a more positive way, everyone would be equally special.

- Initiated a one-year Bible reading program we could all do together.

Nothing in the list above is outstanding or exceptionally creative. That may be the important point here. Going into a situation, new pastor-leaders have a mountain of things to learn. They need time to settle in, figure out who is who, what is what, and where is where. The master plan and specific goals to move the church toward that plan must come later. But, in the meantime, a leader can begin to establish the perception of competency among the people by piling up small wins. They don't have to be big. But, in most cases, new leaders cannot afford to start with colossal blunders during the early months.

Establishing Competency in Daily Living

Remember: all the eyes in the church are on you. The metaphor of living in a glass house or a fish bowl is not paranoia. You are being watched:

- What questions do you ask?

- Whom do you spend time with?

- What do you talk about?

- What gets you excited?

- What seems to disturb you?

- What is on your meeting agendas?

- Whom do you praise?

- What will you criticize?

- How do you spend your money?

- How do you dress?

- How do you interact with your family?

- Do you keep your promises and commitments?

- Do you exaggerate?

- Are you the hero of all your pulpit stories?

- Are you approachable?

- How is your personal hygiene?

- Are you a giver or a taker?

- Are you lazy or a hard worker?

- Are you punctual?

- What type of entertainment do you enjoy?

- What are your hobbies?

- Do you prepare your messages or wing it?

- Do you sing during the services or look bored?

A popular song has these words in the chorus:

I'll be watching you . . .

Every move you make

Every breath you take,

Every thing you do

I'll be watching you . . .

I'm sure I'm taking the song out of context, but at least that portion of it would make a great theme song for pastors. The people in the congregation are watching their pastor. That can either annoy and depress pastors, or they can see the positive. What a tremendous opportunity to make an impact. We have the chance to establish credibility and communicate competence in so many ways every week. Use these ways. Remember that every conversation and encounter with church members is a wonderful time to influence, encourage, minister, serve, and love. Every expression, word, implication, and action is being evaluated. Turn the attention focused upon you to communicate your convictions, commitment, courage, and, yes, competency to do what God has called you to do.

Establishing Competency Through Intentional Risky Ambitions

Not everything we do will be successful. But the better the batting average, the more quickly competency will be established and the more quickly the process of turnaround can be implemented. Remember that there must be perceived alignment between what the leader says and what the results are. The fear of failure is one reason some pastors either a) make the goals too small and, therefore, unexciting or b) postpone risky endeavors indefinitely.

A Note about Risk!

For the past two years I've been asking thousands of pastors and denominational leaders two questions. The first: Do you know of any church that has not been beset with moral failure or doctrinal heresy and has gone bankrupt solely because they took a big step of faith to expand and initiate big ministry projects? So far, I've yet to hear of even one such example.

The second question: How many of you know of any churches who closed their doors because they did not attempt great ambitious things for God but rather allowed themselves to dwindle to the point of nonviability? When I ask this one, hands shoot up all over the room!

How long will it take us to realize that the great sin of the church today is lack of faith? Pastor-friend, do you really think that God will allow you to be the first?

Take a Risk!

Let's just suggest a few illustrations of risky endeavors leaders might undertake in conjunction with their leadership team. Any one of these will help to establish the competency of the pastor to lead. I hope these illustrations cause your creative, risk-oriented juices to flow:

- Take a special offering for a missions project that will accomplish something near to the hearts of your congregation. Make the dollar goal the largest the church has ever attempted. Remind them that for this offering, 100 percent goes directly to the mission need. Make the project specific, personal, and tangible. Remind the people that the mark of a great church is not how much money they take in but how much they can give away.

- Actually meet—or better yet exceed—your budget. This may mean teaching stewardship in a creative manner that has never been attempted before.

- Undertake a building project. Complete a successful three-year building campaign.

- Add more off-street parking and fill the lot.

- When cash flow is behind and funds are low, take the initiative with the board to cut expenditures. Start with your own salary and suggest a plan that will address the realities until this situation is turned around. Lead in the pain. Show confidence in the future.

- Begin a second service. Recruit a musician to help lead it.

- Preach a series of sermons that are memorable for their evidence of study and wisdom.

- Administrate well. Deal with problems. Better yet, look around the corners so you can help the church avoid big problems. There is nothing like two years of peace and tranquility to get people's attention. Be the pastor who resolves conflict and anticipates well.

- Hire well. Fire fast when necessary. Clean up any messes you are responsible for.

- Steadily improve the quality of printed materials.

- Look around the church property and see what improvements can be made without spending a lot of money.

- Counsel well. Mend families.

- Lead some people to faith in Christ and disciple them until they become mature followers of Christ and workers in the church.

You get the idea. Some of these actions cost money. Most do not. The list is endless. The concept is to do something. Do anything to establish your competency to lead. Say what you plan to do and then, above all, *do* it. Strategies, plans, goals—none of these by themselves are effective or particularly impressive. Successful achievement, however, does begin to establish hope in the minds of the people in a turnaround church. "Maybe, just maybe, God can still do something here."

Establishing Competency in Crisis

By definition, crisis is not something you can plan nor something you want to pray for. But crisis will come to all of us. "All must sip the cup of sorrow. I today and you tomorrow." As we give daily attention to our character, we will be equipped to deal with the traumas and challenges of life. Here, however, I want to think with you about what perhaps is one of the few "bright spots" of the dark moments of life.

Remember that everyone is watching the pastor. That is never truer than during times of crisis. They know that when the tea bag hits the hot water what is inside of it comes out.

Pastor Green entered his first church fresh from seminary. He knew a lot about theology, but not much about leadership. Calvary Presbyterian

Church received him warmly. There appeared to be a marriage between pastor and people. The congregation was slightly over the 100 mark in attendance when he was appointed. The people were quite receptive to his emphasis upon reaching the community, nestled in the beautiful Olympic Peninsula.

As the months passed, Calvary experienced impressive growth, much to Pastor Green's surprise and the amazement of all who had belonged to this 45-year-old church. They had peaked 15 years earlier and so were quite amazed that so many people were now coming to hear the "new man in town." They were pleasantly surprised that many came back and even more surprised that 50 new members were added each year for the first two years. There was a steady stream of visitors each week.

One Sunday as the service was about to close, a visitor stood up and began to speak out quite loudly in a manner that no one could understand. The people sat shocked. This was something they had never encountered before. Pastor Green knew immediately from his seminary training that this visitor was probably speaking in tongues. Knowing that he could not allow her to continue, but not wishing to hurt the woman, who was in all likelihood very sincere, he simply spoke to her saying, "Sister, I'm going to ask you to stop!" She did so. The congregation sat in shock, having never seen anything like this. Following the service Pastor Green quickly sought her out and assured her he was not angry with her; he invited her to visit him at his office. When she came, he spent time with her explaining how he understood the Scriptures. He listened while she shared her beliefs. Through their conversation she came to understand the doctrine and worship style of Calvary Presbyterian.

George Manting and his congregation at Willington Assembly always enjoyed the open mic testimonies at their church on Thanksgiving Eve. It was a tradition of the church. All people were free to share what they were thankful for that year. The sharing came spontaneously, and all in attendance felt it to be a meaningful all-church event. Their church had experienced some plateau but was showing signs of health. With three services and new people weekly, it was not unusual for George not to know a person's name and sometimes not to recognize his or her face. So, when a man came in late, stood at the back of the sanctuary for a while listening, and eventually moved to a microphone to take his turn sharing, George thought little of it—that is until the stranger began to speak.

"Are *you* the people who believe in blood?" he bellowed in an angry intimidating manner. "I know what you are all about. He had one hand in a coat pocket. The menacing nature of his voice and the mention of blood frightened everyone in the room.

Pastor Manting responded, "Thank you for sharing here tonight. We're glad you've come to be with us. Is there anything more you need to share or say?"

"Wipe that smile off your face!" the stranger ordered as he continued to approach the platform area.

"We don't mean to offend you," said George. Then addressing a couple of off-duty police officers in the sanctuary, he asked them to come and talk with "our new friend." They did so. He was escorted outside and eventually taken away by the police.

The purpose of these illustrations is simply to give examples of the types of things most pastors will need to deal with at some time in their ministry. These situations cannot be planned, scheduled, or prepared for. The leader must react immediately. What is said, and how it is said, and what is not said all leave lasting impressions. Loss of temper or cool under pressure will color people's impression of you. Maintaining composure under pressure will enhance your competency standing.

Other events which give the pastor a chance to lead are found in what seems to be an ever-increasing series of mega-events. Here are just a few we have experienced recently:

- ◆ The September 11, 2001, terrorist attacks

- ◆ Recession, unemployment

- ◆ War with Iraq

- ◆ SARS

Perhaps as we approach the end times, we should expect wars, rumors of wars, pestilence, and violence. Each time this happens, fear grips the hearts of our people, and they look for a word from God. These are opportunities to display our own confidence in the sovereignty of God, the reality of the Easter message, and our ultimate belief that we need not fear only that which kills the body.

Leadership under pressure speaks of competency because it gives an unplanned insight into:

a. Personal coping mechanisms

b. People skills

c. Public skills

d. Professional leadership skills

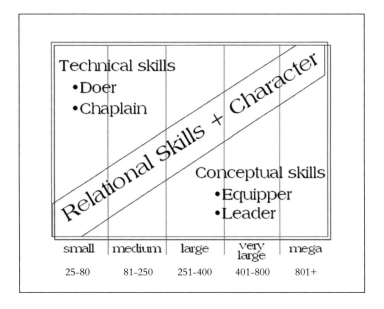

This illustration shows what are essential competencies for a leader in various sizes of congregations. Relational skills and character are constant requirements for all leaders to be effective over time.

CHAPTER 6

Coaching Helps: Competency

By Daniel Harkavy

"For almost 17 years of ministry I have made it a point to continually strive to grow and expand my pastoral and leadership abilities. I faithfully attended conferences and read books on ministry and leadership but there always seem to be one component missing. The pastoral coaching program of Ministry Coaching International was that missing component for me.

"Coaching helped me better understand my personal ministry style and strengths. Now instead of trying to continually change my God-given style, I have learned to embrace it and minister through it more effectively.

"Coaching has helped me stay focused and organized. I can honestly say that I have accomplished more personal and professional growth in the past year than I have ever thought possible. (see figure 4-a) Building His Champions gave me the tools necessary to find deeper significance and success as a husband, father, and minister."

Bob Hulett
King's Way Christian Center, Cape Coral, Florida

> **General Fund Giving** - Prior to coaching was $554,008 projected for 2002 to $645,000. **A 15 percent increase in giving in the first year.**
>
> **Sunday Morning Adult Attendance** - Prior to coaching was 303 and is presently at 366 with total attendance at 500. **A 17 percent increase in attendance in the first year.**
>
> **Lay Leadership** - Prior to Coaching, lay leadership was at 53 and is presently at 110 active in ministry. **A 52 percent increase in lay leadership in the first year.**
>
> **Wednesday Evening Adult Attendance** - Attendance was at 84 and is presently at 103. **An 18 percent increase in attendance in the first year.**

FIGURE 4-A

Competency Is What They See

Competency is the prove-it function of your job. It is what we, your board and congregation, observe in the life of our leader. We see how competent you are when you deliver the Sunday message, lead the board meeting, interact with your staff, and manage the budget. As stated earlier, if you lack convictions, commitment, or courage, operating in the competence zone alone will lead to just short-term success. Your leadership skills must grow in order for you to turn your team and church around. You have two choices when it comes to improving how you grow as a leader: the first is proactive and by design; the second is reactive and by chance.

The Ministry Plan

In the business world, we coach executives to map out their disciplines and their plans. After we assist them with identifying what they do best and how they are to grow their business, we help them order their day around the activities that will enable them to accomplish their objectives. We help them do this by assisting them in creating their business plan. We have identified three key steps to developing an effective business plan. They are very similar to the steps in the Ministry Plan outlined in Chapter Four.

The key steps are:

1. The Numbers or Outcome — Identifying the Goal

2. Identifying the Disciplines

3. Identifying the Improvements

If business leaders nail steps two and three, they will greatly increase the probability of reaching their desired outcome, outlined in step one. The challenge for most is adhering to a calendar that is filled with the activities identified in steps two and three of the business plan.

It is really no different in the church world. As the executive or leader, you have probably been gifted with the skill or experience to do most of what needs to be done in order for the church to run. This problem is compounded when you have the talent to do *all* of the functions with some degree of competence. This can make it very difficult for you to delegate what you need to offload in order to devote more time doing what you are best at. The real question is, Are you investing your time into what the church needs you to be doing in order for the body to grow and people's lives to be changed?

Following are the three steps in developing your Ministry *Plan*:

Step One: The Numbers or Outcome – Identifying the Goal

What is your single most critical goal or objective for the year? Is it a baptism goal, an attendance goal, a decisions goal or a monetary goal? What single outcome will fuel the majority of your action plans for the year? Once this is identified, you and your team will gain clarity on what roles you each need to play. This will also give you clarity in steps two and three of your ministry plan.

Step Two: Identifying the Disciplines

The Disciplines of a Champion© are what we call the top three to six activities that you need to fill your week with. After interviewing several pastors, we have found the following activities to be most critical to their leading their teams and churches effectively: study and lesson time, coaching staff leaders or members, mentoring lay leaders, discipling, planning, elder meetings, and preaching.

This step of identifying the disciplines is greatly clarified in the business world when we ask our clients to tell us how much they want to earn in the year ahead. We then take that number and divide it by the number of working hours in a year, 2080. This gives us their desired hourly wage. Once this is gleaned, we can measure this wage against each activity they participate in during a normal day. We find that many see how they are robbing themselves and their employers by spending too much time doing $10-per-hour work but being paid a $40-per-hour wage.

I challenge you as pastors to do this exercise as well. The church is paying you a wage. Are you spending time doing things that you could offload to volunteers or to individuals who would be happy to take this work for a fraction of the wage? It is not about cheating individuals. It is about understanding that we are not all gifted in the same ways nor do we earn the same wages. We help people when we allow them to volunteer or grow by doing work they were designed to do.

Step Three: Identifying the Improvements

The third step in developing our Ministry Plan is to identify the improvements.

When he started his coaching relationship with Ministry Coaching Int'l, Pastor Rick reported huge frustration with his inability to complete projects. He stated that he had struggled with implementation his entire adult life. Frustrated by the several starts, stops, and drops, he solicited help from a coach. The first real breakthrough came when he was helped to see that he has been less than focused and realistic with what he and his team could do. He is not alone, nor is this a problem that just plagues church leaders. Business leaders can share the same frustrations. We see this problem stemming from two primary challenges.

The first is not having a well-thought-out plan that identifies which projects are most important, what resources are needed, and how much time will be required to bring the projects to fruition.

The second is the lack of a plan and schedule that would lead one to be disciplined with implementation. Recall when you took your first church leadership position. If you were like most, you devoted a substantial amount of time to planning and equipping yourself for this position of huge responsibility. Then success or turmoil followed. With either of these scenarios, the leader is usually thrown into reactive mode. With success comes the busyness that is required to maintain all that is involved with the growth that you are enjoying. This is where the plateau effect hits. Growth stops because the leader and his team are no longer spending time working on new ideas, opportunities, or challenges. The leadership team spends the majority of its time making the slight adjustments or fixes that are required to keep the machine going. The solution to overcoming this problem is found in ON time.

The Four Major Time Categories

Most leaders spend their time in the following four categories:

1. **GROWTH** This time is defined by activities that help you and your organization to grow. In business the growth is quantifiable, as money, numbers, or market share and usually the target of time spent here. For the church leader, it could be preaching, mentoring, discipling, and praying.

2. **IN** This time is defined by activities that come with managing the church. They are the administrative functions you might be involved with. In business we call this "time at the conveyor belt." This could be time spent answering e-mail, returning phone calls, reviewing or writing memos, working on the facility, and so on. Our goal in coaching church leaders is to help them minimize time spent IN the ministry.

3. **ON** This time is defined by activities that help you and your team to improve in knowledge, efficiency, or skill. At Building Champions, we say that ON = Improvement. ON Time could be filled with studying leadership; working on the strategic plan, your teaching plan, or your coaching plan; learning financial management, and so on. ON Time is when you work uninterrupted on the projects that will turn your team and church around.

4. **OFF** This time is critical for the pastor. In a role that often comes with zero boundaries, taking time OFF can be a struggle. As I mentioned earlier, we, your congregation have set such unrealistic expectations on you and your time. If you don't establish a discipline of OFF Time or Sabbath rest, you and your team will be in danger. I know that some of you have not had a full day off in months or a two-week vacation in years. This is not something to brag about, it is something to fix.

Making ON Time a Discipline

You need to clarify On Time to map it out. Competencies improve with the discipline of ON Time. We have found that very few of our new clients have ON Time as a discipline. They used to, but their organizations and teams grew and their ON Time disappeared. ON Time requires you to focus, and focusing is highly difficult for many of us. We have become so used to multitasking that really focusing on just one subject for any length of time can be a challenge. Not only is focusing hard, it is not nearly as fun as talking with our peers about great ideas, projects, or even problems. Many leaders have been gifted with the ability to come up with great ideas, but they lack the discipline of bringing the ideas to fruition.

ON Time works best for me when it is scheduled well in advance, when I have my setting prepared in advance, when I have a realistic goal for each block of ON Time. This is where Step 3 of your Ministry Plan really helps. If you have taken the time to map out the year and as long as there are no significant challenges or opportunities that present themselves, your ON Time projects will be from the plan. You may have identified one major project for the year that needs to be broken down to five minor projects in order to get done.

The 8 Steps to Planning and Allocating the Time for ON Time

Since many leaders have high I behavioral styles (as defined in DiSC language), we have much experience coaching overly optimistic people. The majority of our coaching team have some high I in them as well, so we know what we are talking about on this topic! What is needed is a process for planning and allocating ON Time. Without a process, your chances of implementation success is greatly diminished.

Here is a breakdown of the common approach to project implementation:

The Reality: The leader is overly optimistic and overloaded with projects.

The Mindset: The leader thinks one good ON day will alleviate the pressure.

The Plan: Take all of next Friday to get caught up. Schedule no appointments and get it done.

The Problem: Any normal leader would need 28 hours to complete the targeted projects. The leader comes to his office and fires up his e-mail. He does not protect his time by changing his voice-mail or asking the receptionist to hold his calls. He is interrupted by e-mail and phone calls every 11 minutes. He has not prioritized what needs to be done. He does not have all of his information required to work on his projects in his office. He cannot find three of the critical documents he needs.

The Outcome: Four hours into the day, the leader realizes there is too much to do and feels overwhelmed. The sun is shining and Steven, a new believer, needs to talk about his recent decision for Christ and some struggles he is having. The leader departs with Steven for the golf course, where God can really use him.

The Future: The leader comes back to work feeling anxious and frustrated with the unrealistic amount of work and the lack of progress he is making and jumps back into the day-to-day minutiae of the church. Things do not change, improvements are not made, and there is no turnaround.

The following eight steps will help you establish ON Time, which will in turn help you implement your projects.

Step One: Identify your projects.

Write them all down. Write down every single project that you have committed to completing or that you have the desire to get done.

Step Two: Prioritize your projects by due date and ease of implementation.

Sometimes this step is easy because of the criticalness of your projects. If you have difficulty prioritizing your projects, you can sit down with the team and get their input. This will often help with team member buy-in. Another option is to meet with your board, or a specific board member who is gifted in planning, to help you flesh out your thoughts. The tournament process also works very well.

See below for an example:

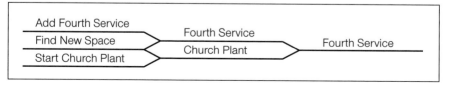

Step Three: Estimate the time required and allocate the tasks.

Most of us fall down here. Estimating and allocating require thinking. Too often we will not think through the process of bringing a project to completion. This is often why contractors fail: in their desire to get the job, they underestimate the hours and materials required to meet the customer's expectations. This can be done only so many times before they underestimate themselves out of business. As leaders, we often do the same thing, and the outcome is no different. When we fail to deliver the goods on time, our teams lose respect for us. Since they perceive that keeping commitments is not important for us, they are less inclined to keep commitments themselves. This is one of the greatest factors in creating a culture of decline.

Any project that will take more than six hours should be broken down into manageable chunks.

The first step in this process is to think through the project. As best-selling author Steven Covey writes, "Begin with the end in mind." What do you want the finished project to look like?

Now, back up from there. What action steps will need to be taken in order to get from here to there?

How much time will each step take? Many leaders tend to be overly optimistic, so we coach them to double the amount of time they think each step will take. There is much more joy when we finish a project early in comparison to the stress that comes from finishing a project past our deadline.

Next, create specific action plans for each action step. Each action plan should fit into a block of time that you can manage.

Leverage your time. Identify who can participate in the process of improving. What action plans can be delegated to others on the team?

Step Four: Create a schedule.

The pastors we coach experience a defining moment regarding their schedule when we help them understand that in order to fulfill their mission *they* need to direct their schedule and time. Most pastors feel they must remain entirely flexible and have open doors at all times to assist people in need. What they begin to realize is that being intentional with their time, practicing time blocking for all appointments and projects, as well as prospecting for lay leaders, actually allows them to reach and minister to larger numbers of people. They then experience greater balance because they are raising up leadership, delegating care, and creating a mobilized, mission-minded army to care for needs and disciple people, therefore fulfilling their calling and mission. This is a beautiful thing!

Pastor Shannon is very optimistic and often struggles with realistically estimating how much time will be needed to bring projects to completion. In the past, he has found himself pulling all-nighters to finish his projects before their deadlines. He also admitted that the quality of his efforts were not his best. We coached him through what we call the chunk-down process, Learning to break bigger projects into smaller objectives.

This project time is ON Time, and it is one of your highest payoff activities. The key here is to actually schedule the action plan time with yourself in advance. If one action plan will take three hours to implement, schedule the three-hour appointment in your calendar and treat it as if it were your most important appointment of the day. This step is key for those who struggle with getting things done.

Step Five: Communicate your schedule.

Your team has to know how important ON Time is to their success and how you must be protected when working ON your projects. Share your schedule with them and then let them know when they will have access to you. If you lock yourself up for the day and they have no idea of when you will come or call in, you will have interruptions throughout the day. Instead, if you will be spending the entire day working ON a project, let your team know, for example, that you will available from 11:00 to 11:30 and from 3:00 to 3:30.

Step Six: Select and prepare your setting

It is daunting to try to get high-altitude insights and work done when your are stuck in the minutiae of your day-to-day demands. Team-member interruptions, e-mail, phone calls, last week's memos—they are all IN Time functions and have a way of sucking you right out of ON Time. Depending on your church facility, you may have a library or a study room. If so, this setting can work well. Gene and I both love doing ON work at the beach. Much of this book is being written at the beach. A home office works well, as does a library or a hotel room. Pick a place or two and set them up for this type of work. Associate the chosen settings with ON Time, which, next to your time in preaching, praying, and studying the word, is your highest payoff time.

Step Seven: Prepare for your ON Time.

You must clearly identify the desired outcome of your ON Time. If you don't, chances are you will not be prepared. What files will you need? What research must be done in advance? What updates do you need from the team? What software, books, or documents will you need? Take the time to prepare in advance for your ON Time.

Step Eight: Execute your ON Time.

It is ON Time. Everything from Satan to your team will attempt to distract you. Old habits will attempt to derail you. This is where commitment shows its head. Remember, it is much easier to continue to do what you have always done than it is to intentionally change and improve. ON Time = Improvements! Be so committed to your ON Time that you will reschedule a lunch appointment with a key member before you will reschedule your ON Time. Without this level of commitment, you will find your ON Time to be greatly compromised and your results to be less than rewarding.

Getting this ON Time discipline down is like going to the gym for the first time in years. If you walk into the gym with no plan and see the huge menu of machines and fit people working hard on them, you may be overwhelmed and give up before you even begin. If your first gym experience includes a tour and a session with the fitness coach, you leave with a plan about what you need to do to reach your fitness goals. You know how much time to spend working on each body part, which machines and how much weight to use. The same is true with ON Time.

Determining How Much ON Time You Need

Now that you have the steps for success outlined, your next decision is to decide how much time you want to spend improving yourself and your team.

One of our coaches shared her frustrations with me about how so many of her team members were struggling with following through with ON Time and getting their projects done. Being a great implementer and one who is totally committed to spending time improving herself on a weekly basis, she could not understand why everyone could not commit a mere one day per week to this discipline.

I asked her when she developed this ON Time discipline and why it started. She replied that when she first started coaching, her ON Time was really reaction time to the major gaps in her organization. When the pain got bad enough, she would assess, brainstorm, and fix whatever was causing the pain. She also admitted that she had been in plateau for three years prior to really learning about and committing to a new ON Time schedule. Her ON Time now takes place all day every Friday. She has been living this discipline now for the last two years, and the growth she and her team have experienced has been phenomenal. She started with two hours every other Friday, which grew to four hours every other Friday, which led to four hours every Friday, and eventually to six and then eight hours every Friday.

Some of our clients have found that committing to Friday afternoons from 1:00 to 5:00 weekly works well. Others are experiencing great results from "First Fridays"—Committing the entire first Friday of each month to ON Time. They will go to an offsite location to work only on the two or three projects that they have defined as being most critical.

Making the Most of ON Time

Setting and tools make the difference.

It was a warm summer morning here in Lake Oswego in 1997. I had been really looking forward to bringing a few projects to completion on this ON Friday. At about 6:30 a.m., I took off from the dock on my boat and set anchor in a nice little cove down the hill from our home. The lake was empty—just me, my Bible, journal, laptop, and God. I was so pumped for this day.

However, within minutes, my excited and overly optimistic state of mind changed to a crazed and hopeless angst. I opened my Bible but had no idea what I was to read. I set the Bible down, went to the rear of the boat, and got down on my knees to pray. But I didn't have my thoughts together, so I really didn't yet know what to ask God for. I jumped up to the seat and fired up my laptop. I thought I just need to see what all I need to get done today. If I can gain clarity on this, then I will be able to pray and seek wisdom from his Word on what projects I need to work on and decisions I need to make.

Can you picture this scene? All of this took place in a matter of ten minutes. I looked like a crazy man! I was a crazy man. I felt like I had sucked down 3 huge cups of fully leaded Starbucks. But God is good, and, just after falling to my knees again and asking him to guide me, my day was salvaged. It was not even close, though, to being one of my more productive ON days. I had no plan, no agenda, no defined end result for the day. I just went out there with my backpack filled and hoped I would be superman in getting it all done.

I have found three settings that work best for me for ON Time. First, I have set up my home study so that it is very conducive for me with ON Time. It is, in fact, my favorite ON Time location. The second setting is at 35,000 feet. I do a fair amount of travel and always turn my flights that are longer than two hours into ON Time. If they are shorter, I will catch up on reading or IN-the-business type of work. The third setting is hotel rooms. When I travel, I set up the hotel room so it works well for me. I very rarely turn on the TV or read the local paper when in a hotel. I have found that using this setting to think, plan, and create can really leverage my travel.

A few years back, I was introduced to Mike Vance and Diane Deacon, authors of *Thinking Outside of the Box and Breaking Out of the Box*. At Apple Computer, Mike had been pivotal in the building of their corporate culture, which has helped to launch the PC revolution. He then became the dean of the Disney Institute, famous for its revolutionary training programs in customer service. He was in charge of Idea and People Development for Walt Disney Productions, Disneyland, and Walt Disney World. Mike and his team were instrumental in creating Disney World in Florida and came up with several of Disneyland's unique offerings. Grad Night and Corporate Nights were two of his ideas. The challenge was to bring in more revenue to the park with a limited number of days in a year and limited space to handle all of the people. Offering the park in off-peak hours was the solution, and now thousands of people visit Disneyland in off-hours due to his outside-of-the-box thinking.

Mike and Diane promote creating positive corporate cultures that foster continuous creativity. What they taught me and thousands of others is the process they call Displayed Thinking™. This process helps you take an idea or situation and break it into linear steps by breaking each detail into bite-sized pieces. (This tool can be purchased from Mike and Diane through the Creative Thinking Association of America at www.creativethinkingassoc.com.)

Creating an ON Time Culture

If you want your team to be cutting edge, they must have discipline. Dave Anderson is in charge of sales and marketing at Building Champions. He is an optimistic guy with an attitude that cannot be topped. Our team is small, with less than 25 members, so each department leader has a fairly wide scope of responsibility. As Dave will admit, this is his strength and his weakness. He lives and breathes what we do and will take on anything that needs to be done in order to further our impact.

There are days when he has so many plates spinning that the slightest breeze will cause one or more to come crashing down. He has told me that this causes him great stress and makes him feel as if he is failing due to being mediocre with many tasks and disciplines instead of being masterful with what is most important. Over the years, he has been coached by me and by Barry Engelman, who is in charge of Coach Development here at Building Champions Int'l.

We have spent several coaching sessions focusing on project management and the discipline of ON Time. I can recall a session last year where Dave came in with several sheets of paper that represented all that he was working on. He was feeling very overwhelmed and could not put his finger on where he was on several of his projects.

The action plan was simple. He needed to leave the office for the next six hours and straighten everything out. This block of ON Time for him was about identifying the status of each of his projects and then mapping out the next action step on those that were not yet complete. He came in the next day greatly relieved with a very strong grasp on all that he had going on. I am greatly pleased now when I see that he is out of the office for an ON Day. What I know is that when he returns, he will be totally on top of it and will have made great progress on our priorities.

CHAPTER 7

Choices

By Gene Wood

Every turnaround leader will of course inherit a team. Most church teams are by definition volunteers. You cannot manage them, but in time a pastor does begin to have a say in choosing the new team and assigning each member in his role.

Fred Smith Sr. is a business leader, churchman, and author of several books on leadership. He once commented to me over breakfast, "When a baseball team has been piling up losing seasons, everyone understands that when a new manager is brought in he needs to bring in some new players." The relevant point here is that when a church has been in demonstrable plateau and decline most people understand that something must change to achieve preferable results.

Collins, in his book *Good to Great*, says it so simply: "Get the wrong people off the bus, the right people on the bus, and then get them in the right seats." That is what this chapter is all about.

The ability of the pastor-leader to achieve a high batting average of successful choices in the selection of paid staff and lay leaders for the turnaround team will either enhance the perceived value of his leadership or irrevocably undermine the confidence of those who follow. No one will bat 1,000 but the turnaround leader will need to be well over .500. So, hire and appoint slowly and fire or remove as quickly as possible.

Who are the right people?

We will talk about aligning four different groups of people within the church:

1. The congregation

2. Lay leaders overseeing ministry teams

3. The official board

4. Professional (paid) staff

Alignment assumes that the leader has established clearly the convictions of the church. One thesis of this book is that once convictions and commitment have been courageously brought to the church, then and only then can a meaningful selection take place.

A 50-year-old evangelical denomination has gone through a series of chief executive officers during the past 15 years. Each of the men appointed has brought unique gifts and energy to the endeavor. But each has left in a dismal parting. Analysis of the denomination reveals that it has failed to clearly define itself—what it is and what it believes. The assumption among the paid personnel, who have the most to lose, is that "we defined who we were 55 years ago, and that should suffice." The problem is that in the absence of open dialogue regarding convictions and goals, the churches, schools, and mission agencies have been free to drift into various directions. The opposite of clear definition and dialogue will always be drift. Herein lies the problem in finding a leader for the denomination. No one involved in a search process has any certain idea of whom to look for.

1. Choosing the Congregation

I suspect that many pastors have never thought about choosing the congregation. When in decline, a church may be preoccupied with getting bodies in the door. This desperation may easily be covered with pious justification. After all, the church doors should be open to everyone. God loves all people. We are not to be judges. Jesus died for all people. "Whosoever will may come."

The above statements are each true, in the right context. But turnaround leaders understand the distinction between the local church and the universal church, which consists of all born again believers.

I would like to suggest a list that I have never seen in print, but I believe is long overdue. This is a checklist of people who should *not join your church*. I'm not saying they should be prevented from attending your church, but they should not be accepted into membership.

- Those who are not Christians.

- Those who are unwilling to go through the prescribed membership procedures to adequately understand what they are getting into.

- Those who are not willing to support the church and its ministries financially.

- Those who have a history of chronic troublemaking and have left their previous church with unresolved conflicts.

- Those who are under church discipline in another church for reasons that have merit, and they have been unwilling to resolve those issues.

- Those who are not willing to subscribe to and support the stated convictions of your church.

- Those who do not plan to have a ministry in your church.

- Those who will not or cannot follow the duly appointed leadership of your church and joyfully trust them to be overseers of their souls.

Let's be clear. Refusal to recruit, wine-and-dine, woo, and court someone into a local church is not tantamount to excluding them from heaven. In most every case there are plenty of options, other local assemblies, where perhaps they would fit better, serve more enthusiastically, grow more quickly, worship more sincerely, give more sacrificially, be more joyful, and in the end please God more fully. Isn't that the goal?

Turnaround leaders understand the need to begin building a healthy team by receiving into membership those who are aligned with the convictions and commitments to their local church.

Just say NO . . . a new church growth trend.

Wait a moment, you say. If 70-85 percent of all the Protestant churches in United States are plateaued or in decline, how do we help ourselves by steering people elsewhere? The empirical evidence, however, supports the thesis that when leaders begin to accept that their church is not for everyone, their church begins to become inviting and attractive to more.

For example, doctrine has become almost a dirty word in some churches. But Thom Ranier reports in his book *High Expectations* that in the fastest-growing churches they studied, three out of ten *required* agreement with their doctrine to join and another six out of ten *expected* the same. I suggest that the more latitude of convictions a church allows, the less ability it will have to attract and secure high levels of support from its members. I have become increasingly convinced this is one of the reasons entire denominations are suffering today.

Trend Letter magazine (November 11, 2002) reported:

> What began as a trickle turned to a flood of boomers returning to the religious institutions of their youth. . . . Interestingly, in the United States, conservative religious groups that demand high financial and emotional commitment from the membership grew faster than more moderate denominations in the last decade" (p. 8).

In our new members class, I close the four weeks with what I call a "personal word from the pastor." I share that it seems silly to me for anyone to join Grace Church unless they plan to do four things:

1. Serve. Find a ministry which fits your spiritual gifts and be busy sharing those gifts for the good of this body.

2. Engage in stewardship. And I spell it with a dollar sign.

3. Join a small group. You are expected to be in a small group or class where you know others and are known on a more intimate level.

4. Submit to leadership. Why join a church where you don't believe the leaders care for you and can be trusted? This does not imply questions cannot be asked, but an atmosphere of trust should precede membership.

Will everyone join?

Of course not. But as has so often been stated, by making the expectations of members clear, we get to choose which newcomers we keep and which ones we lose. We can also help steer people to another place where they will be even more happy and effective.

Do we tell people to leave?

Leaders take many different approaches, but I have learned the hard way that for two reasons it is best to not actually tell someone to leave the church. First, most pastors do not have the legal authority to tell someone to leave. A turnaround leader does not bluff. So why assume authority that everyone knows we do not have nor, in most cases, should have? The issue is not one of solving problems but working hard to avoid future problems. So, over the years we want to gather a group of people together who share common convictions and commitments. This team will be an instrument for growth and community impact. But volunteers on a church team must be walking in real harmony, not surface harmony.

In recent years, I have had increasing opportunity to partner with Christians in the open church in China. As a good friend, I have worked hard to learn the culture of the Chinese people. One thing they value highly is surface harmony. They will go to great lengths to avoid having to say no even if no is the ultimate answer to a proposal. They will more likely say, "What you are asking could be very difficult" or "I will talk this over with my people." Another favorite conflict-avoidance technique is silence. The first time or two I encountered this polite silence, I thought perhaps the language barrier had caused them not to hear my question. But they had heard my question very well. Usually the question is phrased in such a manner as to only allow for a simple yes or no. And they, not wishing to say no and cause me to lose face, adopted the best option of silence.

This is what I mean by "surface harmony." A turnaround church, however, must achieve deep harmony. When the congregation is buying the convictions and commitments, then they can actually afford to experience rippling of the waters.

Second, whenever a pastor tells people they need to attend and worship elsewhere, all that gets out regarding the conversation is that Pastor Wells is telling people to get out! And that simply does not play well with anyone.

One approach a pastor might take is similar to that of Rev. Belleflower after he listened to Rick and Jane (age 33).

"For the past hour now I have listened to the many concerns the two of you have with the beliefs and practices of Center Union Church. Let me see if I can recall some of the things you have expressed.

a. You wish that my preaching were less expository and more topical.

b. You would like to see a greater variety of musical expression.

c. You wish that I would preach from the New King James instead of the New International Version.

d. You are not happy that some of our members are wearing blue jeans to church.

e. You think that we should baptize by immersion instead of allowing for sprinkling.

f. You think we should have cell groups in homes instead of maintaining Sunday school as a primary small group format.

"I hope that I've listened to you well. I want you to know that I'm glad you came in to see me today. You've certainly thought through these matters. But you also need to understand that the leadership of Center Union, of which I'm a part, is really committed to how we are doing things here. We have spent much time working out our convictions and philosophy of ministry, master plan, and goals. So, it's important that you understand these matters are not likely to change. In fact some of the things you mention are so important to me, I would be unable to remain here if they changed.

"I want you know that at Center Union, we want to hear from our people and never want to give the impression that thoughtful input is not welcome. But you also need to know that being heard and getting your own way are not synonymous. Each person at Center Union is valuable. And we know that people such as you contribute to the church in many ways, but just because someone buys a ticket does not mean they get to fly the plane.

"We have a unified and capable leadership team at Center Union, and, together, we have defined what we believe and who we are, and have prayerfully articulated where we are going and how we hope to get there. I'd be happy to explain these matters to you, but you need to know the way things are now is not likely to change. Now, do you have further questions?"

"Pastor Belleflower, what do you think we should do? Are you saying we should leave? Do you want us to leave?"

"No, Rick and Jane. I do not want you to leave. I think you should stay right here at Center Union and grow. Frankly, I preach the way I do because I think it is the best way to preach. I also think that the dreams we have for this church are going to provide an exciting impact on not only our own members but our community, and I'd hate to see you miss out on being a part of it."

"Well Pastor, you've given us something to think about. "

"Okay, let's have a word of prayer, and I hope you make the right decision."

See how different that approach can be from telling someone they need to find another church. Everyone is welcome, but to be involved they will need to understand what they are buying into. This is the way a turnaround leader begins to choose the right congregation.

2. Choosing Lay-staff

Volunteers are a gold mine. I encourage you to take an hour to do the following exercise. Make a list of every volunteer position in your church. Add up the hours given in service each week. Now put a $10.00 per hour calculation to each hour. For every 40 hours of cumulative time add $500 for medical insurance and another $200 for workman's comp. What is the total dollar value of your volunteer force? That, however, is only the beginning. Add to that the total giving for the year. That total figure represents the raw monetary value of your volunteer staff.

Next, consider the fact that the Lord has provided divine enablement to each believer. That is their spiritual gift which is bestowed upon each Christian expressly for the benefit of the local church. I am not sure how to value a supernatural ability, but suppose factoring it in at $100.00 per hour would be conservative. (Note: This only holds true, however, if we have the right people in the right place doing the right things, considering their spiritual abilities.) Add these dollar figures to the above man-hours.

Finally, we must consider "executive salaries." Such a valuable workforce requires supervision and oversight to keep the team moving together. These are the ones we'll refer to as the "lay staff." In many churches they are "elected" to a leadership position for one, two, or three years. These positions may include church treasurer, financial secretary, Sunday school superintendent, choir director, trustee, missions chairperson, or similar title.

Whatever the titles may be, the people in their positions are assumed to hold some overseeing, guiding, coordinating, supervising, or leading role. Why not train and equip these men and women to become true leaders? They can be treated like a lay staff team.

Unfortunately, in too many churches these positions are assumed by tenure. A name and a position are held by some individual simply because they have always done it, even if the role has not been performed with purpose, excellence, growth, and vision. A turnaround church needs to take a hard look at who is doing what.

Effective turnaround leaders do not make many of the decisions in the church, but they *do want to decide who makes which decisions.* That is the task of the leader. There are not many hills worth dying on (apart from those having to do with convictions), but this may be such a hill.

Getting the right people in the right seats is critical. In churches run largely by lay volunteers/leaders, the pastor must begin to work immediately to make sure every player on the team knows what their position is and what is expected of them.

The book *The Performance Factor* gives six characteristics of a high performance team. The second is Crystal Clear Roles (p. 35-36).

> "High-performance teams are characterized by crystal clear roles. Every team member is clear about his or her particular role, as well as those of the other team members. Roles are about how we design, divide, and deploy the work of the team. While the concept is compellingly logical, many teams find it very challenging to implement in practice. There is often a tendency to take a role definition to extremes or not take it far enough. However, when they get it right, team members discover that making their combination more effective and leveraging their collective efforts is an important key to synergistic results."

Once we have people aligned to the convictions, philosophy, and strategy of our church, then we make certain they understand the arena they are responsible for and empower them to do the work which they have been assigned to do.

Over the years, I've discovered two types of lay leaders who are especially challenging to work with. The first is the willing but incompetent worker. Some positive characteristics of these people include the following:

- They are faithful and dependable.

- They are agreeable and affable, willing to serve when asked.

- They always listen politely when instructions and suggestions are given as to how the work might be done more effectively.

- They are present whenever the doors are open.

- They are pleasant to be around.

On the challenging side, however, are these qualities:

- They are convinced that the way things have been done for the past 20 years is the best way to do things, perhaps, the only way to do the ministry they oversee.

- Listening does not mean they are learning.

- They seem quite content with the status quo and cannot understand the need or urgency for change.

- They are not creative or adventuresome.

- They can be passive-aggressive in their nonresponsiveness.

The second challenging lay leader is on the other end of the personality spectrum. On the apparent positive side of the ledger are these qualities:

- They are at the church every time the doors are open.

- They openly seek the position they hold; they assume it is their entitlement due to tenure.

- They are hard workers.

- They can be sacrificial with their time, energy, and even financial resources.

- They appear willing to learn and grow in their role and even willing to attend outside seminars and to read books in the area. In fact, they may fancy themselves as experts in the area of service.

But these qualities are countered by these qualities:

- ◆ They will be personally affronted if someone else is asked to fill the position.

- ◆ They do not seem satisfied with ministering and leading in their assigned area of ministry. They feel they must be involved in every aspect of ministry.

- ◆ They take such ownership of the ministry they oversee that they tend to view every church decision based solely upon how it will affect what they care about. In short, their area of ministry is the church. At this point they can become extremely irrational, because of an inability to see a larger picture.

- ◆ Their total self-esteem and self-worth appear to be wrapped up in this one area of service.

Let's remember that we are talking about stagnant or declining churches. Were these people leading ministries that were thriving and positively influencing the larger church context for growth and expansion, then some of their idiosyncrasies might well be overlooked. Too often these lay leaders think they are the right people in the right seat, but they are not. In fact, they may need to give up their seats so the right person can be put in place.

Leading a volunteer force must be one of the most difficult responsibilities in the world today. As mentioned at the beginning of this chapter, the same people we lead are the ones who give the resources necessary for the church to function. The pastor-leader does not write their paycheck, but in fact they write his. It is an extremely delicate balance.

The fact is that the team must accept leadership from their pastor. Teams are, in the truest sense, volunteers. Volunteers are not managed, but they will respond to the recommendations, suggestions, and vision of a leader they trust in ways that defy rational explanation.

Following are some miscellaneous thoughts and suggestions on choosing a lay team:

- ✔ Attempt to make whatever changes are necessary as gently as possible. Avoid hurting well-intentioned servants.

✔ Find out whether the lay leader currently serving is capable of taking things to the next step.

✔ Find out if there is a way to work around an incompetent but faithful, well-intentioned person. Can you give them an assistant? Can you form a task force to do some things they are not able or interested in doing?

✔ Be willing to confront people who over step their assigned arenas of responsibility.

✔ Make very clear what each person's ministry description entails and, as important, what it does not involve. Help them see how what they do complements the larger picture.

✔ Create a culture in which flexibility is admired and affirmed.

✔ Remind people that the ministry is not about having their needs met, but rather meeting the needs of others.

✔ Be aware that most long-tenured positions in a local church are quite likely performed by someone whose identity, esteem, and social needs are being met by the position.

✔ Be prepared to make necessary changes. Deal with problems sooner rather than later.

✔ Affirm capable lay leaders who are displaying personal growth and the understanding that what worked five years ago is probably in need of creative upgrading.

✔ Treat your quality volunteer staff as solid gold. Invest money and time in equipping them for excellence and providing the tools necessary for effectiveness.

3. Choosing Board Members

If a church governing board and pastoral staff are united, it is virtually impossible to experience a debilitating church split. This assures the local church of stability and security. Positively, when the board and staff are united in spirit, the chances of turnaround grow exponentially. So the selection of board and staff are of paramount importance. This section addresses board selections; Section 4 addresses staff selection.

The following thoughts, suggestions, and recommendations are based on decades of personal experience, conversations with other pastors (which could fill volumes), and up-close observations of trauma and victory in congregations across North America. What follows may sound unfair and less than charitable to some good lay people and would-be church board members. I have no desire to hurt anyone or exclude them from leadership or use of their spiritual gifts, but for reasons which will be given, caution should be given when considering some individuals for nomination or appointment to the church governing board.

1. Is the person being considered a worker?

   Since people do what people see and board members are recognized leaders in any congregation, it is critical that they show evidence of the heart, attitude, and discipline of a church worker. I am always leery of those who say they have the gift of leadership or administration and therefore eliminate themselves of any obligation to serve the church in any capacity other than board member or some similar high-profile governing position. In fact, most good leaders have long ago learned how to be good followers. They understand the necessity of someone being in charge and, frankly, often welcome the situation where that someone is not them.

   We have discovered it is healthy for board members to have specific ministry assignments within the church. Not only are they required to make decisions from time to time which affect others, but they are in the trenches in one manner or another.

   Years ago Frank Tilapaugh, in *Unleashing the Church*, noted that there is a huge gap in the thinking between rear-echelon bureaucrats and the front-line troops. On the front line, the soldiers are talking about survival, safety, watching the backs of their comrades, the best way to gain victory, and life and death. There is an intensity of purpose. In the rear echelon, the soldiers are usually complaining about the food and how hard the beds are, and wondering why they don't have more time off and why the television doesn't pick up more sports channels.

   Staying on the front line of ministry ensures that those making decisions are:

   a. in touch with reality and

   b. perceived as credible by the troops fighting the battle.

Colin Powell suggests that a healthy organization should always push the decision making as close to the front line of those who must implement the decisions as is practical and possible. By requiring that all board members be in active ministry, we will improve the likelihood of effective decisions being made.

2. Are they committed to this local church?

   Somewhere along the way, "church speak" has substituted the term *kingdom* for *local church*. I'm not sure whether this reflects some paradigm shift in eschatology or hermeneutics, or if it is due to lack of clear thinking. I suspect the parachurch movements have handed the vocabulary shift to us. Many parachurch agencies and movements obviously choose to work interdenominationally (and this is not wrong or bad). These movements focus on a specific aspect of ministry, such as discipleship, leadership training, the family, Scripture memory, child evangelism, or development of godly men. Their purpose thus makes "kingdom" focus appropriate.

   But the same focus for a local church, while sounding modern and noble, seems to be misguided. The New Testament talks much more often about the local church than it does the invisible church. Some people, including myself, believe that God's primary means for reaching the world is in fact the *local* church. Other movements and agencies, as good as they are, will all come and go, but the institution of the local church will remain until the Lord comes to take us to heaven.

   Therefore, it is necessary to have church board members who are committed to the particular local church they are helping to lead. One way this will be reflected is in where they choose to give their tithe. If Christians want to give to the kingdom, and their heart's desire is to build the kingdom, then it makes logical sense that they go serve on the board of the kingdom wherever that is. And, frankly, I am a little confused as to where they are located.

3. Are they working for a parachurch organization? If so, can they commit to making the local church their number-one priority?

   When talking once with Fred Smith Sr. about serving on boards, he commented (mostly in jest, I think), "Yes, Gene, whenever we are asked to serve on a board, they really want to know two things: 'First, how much money can you give? Second, whom do you know who might be able to give?'"

Now, that is not completely true, but there is an element of truth in it. Board members can make a valuable contribution to the church if they can contribute:

a. in an unusual way financially;

b. in some exceptional manner with expertise, connections, or knowledge; and

c. with their time and service to the church.

The church will accept one of the three, but really needs each board member to contribute in at least two of the three ways.

Sometimes leaders of parachurch organizations are thought to be able to bring exceptional insight and knowledge regarding the church. In reality, the function, work, and development of a local church has some similarities with Christian parachurch organizations, but the differences probably outweigh the similarities. This is also one reason that sometimes successful pastors are unable to make a maximum contribution to parachurch boards.

Due to the normal and reasonable expectations that parachurch organizations put on their personnel, it is almost too much to ask for those same people to give an equal or greater contribution to their church. They already have a ministry where they work. They often feel the need to contribute financially at work to projects they helped to create and feel deeply about. Most effective parachurch leaders already work over and above the paid work hours at their organizations.

The reality is that too often such individuals will eventually feel some degree of conflict of interest and passion. Usually, though not always, their parachurch work will win. The worst-case scenario is when such church board members begin to use their influence and authority on the board to lobby the church for the causes and interests of the parachurch agency.

I am not saying that anyone who works for a parachurch organization will not make a good church board member. There are probably many examples to the contrary. I am suggesting that the senior pastor consider these realities as board choices are made.

4. Have they received some formal educational training for pastoral ministry, do they openly or secretly wish they were a pastor, or have they attempted to pastor and failed?

A wise retired pastor shared that after four decades of ministry, he concluded it unwise to place an ordained individual on the board. There is certainly no biblical reason to make this a policy. But anecdotal evidence seems to indicate some wisdom in this.

Usually when such persons find themselves out of full-time local church service, they believe that they can "really understand what the pastor is going through." This would seemingly make them the perfect candidates for a church board. They often have above-average knowledge of the Bible and of church life, and often have good speaking or teaching capability.

The question is this: When people have held the role of spiritual leader and think like a senior pastor, can they ever stop thinking like a senior pastor? Some can. Most cannot. It may appear that my words are mean-spirited and unreasonable. But they are simply offered to prevent repetition of what is a common sad story.

Perhaps it will help if I make a confession. I have learned over the past decade that it is increasingly difficult for me to serve on a board. Once you begin to think like the leader, it is hard to turn it off and on. I know it would be impossible for me to stop thinking like a pastor. For that reason, I simply could not serve on a church governing board.

So, how do we use people with such leadership experience and giftedness? Here are a couple of suggestions. First, we can have them lead task forces. A task force has a specific objective. When the task is accomplished, the role is ended. Second, they can be used as consultants. You may wish to actually put them on staff at a $1 per year salary. Make them your personal consultant for any area in which they excel: finances, human resource management, computers, teambuilding, training, worship, building, and so on. The key is to communicate that their role is directly related to the senior pastor. You will call them when you need their expertise. Their counsel will be valued and always considered. But in the end, you will make the decisions. What you seek is the privilege of being able to be transparent with them, often providing confidential information necessary for wise advice. However, their role will be limited to their areas of expertise.

5. Are they an entrepreneur-business owner?

See the answer to question 4. Business owners will naturally think like an owner. They do not, nor will they ever, own the church. The dissimilarities between a privately owned business and a local church are greater than the number of similarities. Many godly businessmen understand the differences. Others do not.

6. Are they a good example to the body?

- Are they faithful in giving?

- Do they participate actively and enthusiastically in worship? What are their facial expressions? Do they use their Bible? Take notes?

- Do they greet new people, or do they limit fellowship and social life to a small group of friends?

- Do they know how to just be one of the group or must they dominate every conversation and gathering?

- Are they an oppositional thinker, the predictable odd-man out on a vote, or the last one to be convinced?

- Do they have warm people skills?

- Are they able to manage their children?

- Does their wife respect their decisions and speak highly of her husband?

- Do they know what the direction, philosophy, doctrine, and goals of the church are, and are they supportive of them?

Most important, every board member should display the qualities as set forth in 1 Timothy 3 and Titus 1. They should consistently manifest the fruit of the spirit (Galatians 5:22-23). All of the other issues I've discussed above are intended to be additional and less frequently articulated matters to consider in selection of a board. This section is meant to prompt the leader and nominating committees (as applicable) to consider some common-sense matters in governing board selection. Why go looking for problems?

4. Choosing Staff Members

Some of the discussion in this section may not be immediately relevant to many smaller churches. However, we decided to include it for several reasons. First, the general principles regarding the development of a paid staff team are somewhat transferable in regards to building a volunteer team. Second, if the principles of *Leading Turnaround Churches* and *Leading Turnaround Teams* are faithfully applied, the smaller church will quite likely grow and need to give consideration to hiring staff in time. Finally, most churches over 150 hire at least some part-time staff. The approach and philosophy that drive the first hire will often become part of the church culture.

Another reason a book on team building cannot neglect discussion regarding staff is, simply, it is too important. A united staff and board are not luxuries in a healthy church; they are an absolute nonnegotiable necessity. The board and staff are the leaders of a church. The people look to them to incarnate the relational aspects of Christianity. It is not too strong to suggest that in time the entire congregation will embody the attitude, atmosphere, vocabulary, and behavior patterns they see taking place between the staff and board.

The staff covenant used in our church in Glendora is contained in Appendix C. Reading it will clarify much of what we refer to in this chapter. I am not in any way suggesting this covenant is transferable to all churches—perhaps not for any other church. The purpose of including it is to encourage each senior pastor and board to have the courage to put on paper both the philosophy that drives them and the ethics, boundaries, and values that will define them. Every member of a team deserves to be informed before they are hired, not afterward. Be bold enough to put the too frequently unspoken issues on paper.

Policy versus Administration

As per figure C-2 in Appendix C, it appears reasonable that the governing board of a church best focuses on policy that sets the bounds in which the church can function. Church boards are not usually the best choice to administrate the day-to-day operations of a church unless, of course, it is so stagnant that not much is happening and no new or creative programs are being implemented. Several reasons boards are not the best choice for overseeing the daily functions of the church include:

a. They are usually not selected or elected because of their perceived ability to administrate the church. In most churches, people are placed on the board because they are thought to be very spiritual individuals. One would hope that those responsible for appointing board members (committee or congregation) would have given at least some degree of consideration to the qualities set forth in Titus 1 and 1 Timothy 3.

b. In some cases, board members are elected to the position because they are a long-time member of the church and it would hurt their feelings if they were not on the board.

c. In other cases, people are placed on the board because they have a prestigious title or career outside the church.

d. In worst-case scenarios, people are placed on the governing board of the church simply because they are such "nice" people—without considering any other qualifications.

e. There are too many people on the board to act in an administrative capacity. As Collins points out in *Good to Great*, effective organizations are not noted for *one* big critical and genius decision. These organizations are great because of the dozens of right decisions made each day. Such activity can only be carried out by the pastor and his staff, who are available to act and react throughout the week.

f. It is not reasonable or practical to call a meeting of the board each time an operational decision must be made.

g. Healthy churches are created when the decision makers have the information necessary to make many small decisions with much wisdom. In truth, day-to-day leadership of a congregation is more a learned skill than a science.

h. Lay leaders usually have not had the opportunity for formal training in theology, pastoral practice, counseling, or communications. The task of church ministry is indeed a specialty.

i. Boards take a long time to make good decisions. Therefore, they operate best when called upon to make few decisions, but those decisions that make a *significant* difference in the future of the church.

What are significant decisions? Well, they might be summarized as policy matters. Indeed it is important for the board to set boundaries and determine expectations.

FIGURE 7-A

Hiring Guidelines

Hire slowly—try not to fire at all. This is a twist on Collins's advice (*Good to Great*) where he suggests that corporate leaders should hire slow and fire fast. A better goal in the local church and most nonprofit endeavors is to hire slow and try very hard to never fire anyone.

It is certainly advisable to take whatever time is necessary to make a wise choice in staff selection. Haste may prove unrecoverable in a turnaround church. The larger the staff, the better chance you have to recover from a wrong choice. The need for right choices increases exponentially for smaller staffs.

Many things that have a potential for good have a proportional potential for hurt and pain. Likewise, the choice of staff is never neutral. The person brought onto the team either brings a positive or negative overall impact on the team.

How do you know whom to hire? Bill Hybels has suggested three considerations:

1. *Character.* Most everyone agrees this is the number one factor for a good hire. If character is intact, most everything else can be overcome in one manner or another. More important, if character is not present, then nothing else really matters.

2. *Competency*: See the section below titled "The Job Description" (page 131).

3. *Chemistry*: This is the great intangible. Basically, when you are building the team, you ask yourself, "When this person enters the room, do I most often feel energized and enthused, or drained?"

I would like to suggest one more factor:

4. *Configuration*: See Figure 7b and 7c. The jigsaw philosophy of staffing suggests that no senior pastor is perfectly well rounded. Rather, we each are more like irregularly shaped jigsaw puzzle pieces. That is, we each have strengths and weaknesses. If one accepts the assumption that the staff should be built around the strengths and weaknesses of the senior pastor, then the process is simplified. Go find people who can do well in areas where you do poorly or don't like to do at all.

Two rather obvious issues, unfortunately, are not so obvious to many. First, senior pastors may or may not be able to accurately identify their own weaknesses and strengths. When that occurs, the board often feels the need (though this is seldom specifically articulated) to get involved in the hiring process. Second, when the church (or pastor) believes the senior pastor is a perfectly well-rounded person, competent to do all aspects of pastoral ministry with excellence, then they will be tempted to find another smaller version of the omni-gifted senior pastor.

However, not only is the perfectly rounded senior pastor a myth, but too often a person of similar gifts and weaknesses is hired—thus making one of them unnecessary and sometimes compounding the weakness. In time two or more staff members desire to have the same roles and responsibilities, and competition ensues. This seldom ends well. The point is that we must hire to our weaknesses, not our strengths. This builds a complementary team in which all the members are functioning primarily in their arena of strength and effectiveness, they are effective, and contented.

Mythical concept of the perfect, well-rounded senior pastor

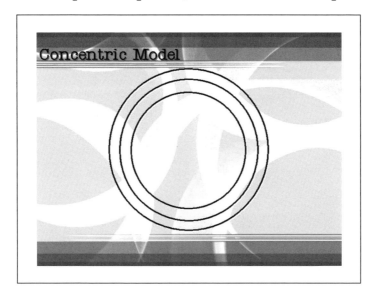

FIGURE 7-B

The assumption of the jigsaw philosophy is that churches build around the shape of their senior pastors. They are not perfectly rounded individuals as shown in Figure 7-b, but have strengths and weaknesses, illustrated by the strange shape of a jigsaw puzzle piece (see Figure 7-c). Pastor-leaders should not seek to find someone like themselves, but rather someone who complements them. The passions, abilities, interests, and training of the new staff will be in the areas where the senior pastor is weak (or as the church gets larger, areas where the senior pastor can no longer make a priority).

Realistic concept. Built around the senior pastor's strengths and weaknesses

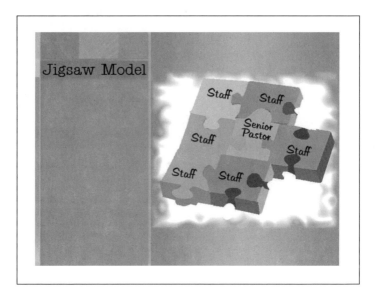

FIGURE 7-C

To build a staff in this manner has several implications:

a. In time you'll gather a rather peculiar assortment of people. Each will be unique in his make-up, perspectives, and interests.

b. You may not have the best staff parties. Normally a good party happens when you bring a somewhat similar (homogeneous) group together. Often they are close to the same economic, educational, and life-stage plane. However, the jigsaw staff will be diverse. But we are not planning a party; we are hoping to turnaround a church.

c. Because of the diversity, the group may not spend as much time together socially outside work as some other groups do.

d. The group members will tend to be more content in their functions because they sense they are needed. What they do well, no one else on the team can compete with.

e. The team will stay together longer than the average longevity of other staff teams. Even though they may not have the social camaraderie of other teams, they will develop a family feel. (Have you ever known an extended family that did not have some odd ducks?)

f. The team members will suffer from some degree of isolation because each must work more independently. This requires the leader to work hard at bringing them together in intentional ways.

g. The team will not suffer the wrench of competition because basically no member desires to do what others are doing. Jealousy and jockeying for position are minimized.

h. The team members will have a sincere appreciation for the strengths of their fellow members. They realize how badly the gifts and abilities of the others are needed.

i. The leader will need to keep the big picture in front of the team so they are aware of the overall wins of the team and how what they are doing is contributing to the objectives and purpose of the church.

Values and Expectations

Be crystal clear as to values and expectations before hiring. We cannot be too clear about what will be expected of new staff *before* they make a decision to come. This must include a list of things important to the senior pastor whether they be biblical, cultural, or ethical, and whether they represent values, or nonnegotiable idiosyncrasies.

In many ways this is like a marriage. Why get married only to fight for the next five decades? Indeed, honesty is the best policy. Here are some things to talk over before a decision is made:

a. Is promptness a high value?

b. What dress codes are required? Expected?

c. What time is the staff expected to arrive in the morning?

d. What type of lifestyle is acceptable?

e. Is a spouse expected to be actively involved in the church?

f. Are children expected to participate in the church programs?

g. Is attendance at staff meetings mandatory?

h. What are the policies and procedures when one is sick? Taking vacation? Personal days?

i. Are they expected to work in the office? If so, how long?

j. What expectations are there regarding worship services? Sunday school?

k. What support staff, if any, will they have?

l. Whom do they report to? Senior pastor? Board? Other?

m. How will their pay be determined each year?

The one hiring owes it to prospective staff to be clear if there are cultural expectations peculiar to the local situation. What are the values the church holds that will ultimately affect promotion, pay, recognition, and ensuring a long-term fit?

The following is an illustrative listing of values that some nonprofit organizations see as priorities but seldom lay on the table at the time of hiring. Which half-dozen should you flag for future team members?

❏ Positive attitude

❏ Smiling

❏ Punctual arrival

❏ Time accountability

❏ Promptness at appointments

❏ Formal/casual dress

❏ Modest dress

❏ Family welcome/not welcome at work

❏ Available 24/7

❏ 24-hour turnaround on phone calls

❏ Willing to work outside job assignment

- ❏ Family active in church: what level?

- ❏ Spouse's involvement in church

- ❏ Conduct of family members

- ❏ Doctrinal issues

- ❏ Sick policy

- ❏ Vacation policy

- ❏ Clean-desk policy

- ❏ Acceptable vocabulary

- ❏ Acceptable ethical behavior

- ❏ What will prompt termination

- ❏ Minimum commitment you seek from them (years)

- ❏ How they should handle grievances

- ❏ To whom do they report

- ❏ Open-door policies

- ❏ Computer usage/accountability

- ❏ Basis of job evaluation

Hiring from Within

What are some advantages to hiring from within the church?

1. You already have a relationship with the new staff member. You know whether you can work with him. This addresses the chemistry issue.

2. The prospective staff member has a good idea as to whether he or she respects the senior pastor and shares the vision and direction of the church.

3. The competency issue can sometimes be evaluated ahead of time.

4. The person knows "the way we do church here." An increasing number of healthy churches have openly admitted they are less concerned about formal theological education and seminary training for most of their staff members than they are about them understanding "how we do things."

5. Inside persons have already demonstrated their commitment level to the particular local church.

6. Cost savings exist because there is no need to move a family into the area.

7. The children (if any) do not need to relocate.

8. There are existing networks of relationships, which can be a great help in recruiting volunteers.

9. The learning curve of a new job is shortened. There is no need to unlearn a way of functioning from a previous ministry.

10. The new staff member already has a sense of the community, culture, and mores.

Disadvantages of Hiring From Within Include:

1. Inside prospective staff members may have a difficult time with the new way of doing things if they have an intense loyalty to a previous pastor. Be cautious if the prospective staff member:

   a. Came to personal faith in Christ under the direct leadership and discipling of a previous pastor. They may subconsciously feel that following a new approach to ministry is a form of disloyalty to the one who brought them to Christ.

   b. The person being considered has been in lay leadership at a significant level during an extended period of decline and plateau. If the person led the church in decline, why should we anticipate he will lead it in turnaround? In fact, he may feel a need to defend what was done during the decline.

2. They may have extended family and close friends who are actually responsible in part for the church's decline. What influence will this have on their work?

3. They may have had experiences from previous years that were effective then, but will prove ineffective today. Can they understand that what worked yesterday may be irrelevant now?

4. Are they willing to lose close friends if necessary to help the church turn around?

5. Some positions do mandate formal theological education and training. It is often difficult to find those people within the church.

6. Jealousy can arise when someone is hired from within.

7. "A prophet has no honor in his or her own country."

8. A layperson may not have had the privilege of broad exposure to what is happening in the wider circle of Christianity.

9. The layperson who comes on staff may tend to "go native" faster than someone from outside. This figure of speech alludes to the outsider who goes into a primitive village to assist them with their quality of life. Initially they are of great benefit to the village as they introduce all the benefits of technology, hygiene, and medicine. But if they stay long enough, the peer pressure of the village begins to take its toll. In time the outsider, seeking to be accepted, becomes more like the villagers and in so doing loses sight of the goal in going there which was to bring positive change.

10. If the hire does not work out and dismissal is necessary, the ripple affect can be devastating.

Job Descriptions

Churches often form a committee to find staff people. This is already a mistake. The pastor should select the pastoral team. If Collins is correct, and I think he is, the key is to get the right people on the bus and let them help us figure out what needs to be done.

What is the painstaking job description process all about? We begin with what our senior pastor's strengths are. Assess what qualified laypeople in the church can do exceptionally well, and then go find someone to supplement what is missing. Of course, some obvious priority decisions need to be made. Do we want to focus first on music/worship, youth, children, clerical, custodial, or some other area? Once that decision is made, a church should seek to find the best person. Period.

We make sure the person can agree with the doctrines and values of the church, fit into the church's culture, and work under the pastor—then hire that person.

Write the job description for the right person. That is, once they have agreed to come, put together a simple outline that fits their gifts, abilities, passions, personality, and core assignments. A goal is to assure that at least 80 percent of what they must do coincides with what they want to do and can do well. No one in the real world gets to do *only* what they want to. I've occasionally told team members, "If you ever find such a job, please get two of them: one for you and one for me." In the Lord's work, ideally we'd do 80 percent of what we do for free (if we were independently wealthy). The other 20 percent is what we're paid to do. A worthy goal for ministry retirement might be to keep doing the 80 percent for free, to give back to the Lord and his church, and be able to say "no thank you" to the 20 percent.

Everything else that is not assigned to another paid staff member will be delegated to volunteer workers—where it already was before the new team member was hired. Everybody wins. Write the ministry assignment around the person.

When Not to Hire Someone

Leith Anderson once said, "A church should never hire someone because they need the job, but only because the church needs them."

Hire slowly and try not to fire at all.

Firing Guidelines: Exceptions and Other Options

In the "Hiring Guidelines" section, we recommended "Hire slowly—and try not to fire at all." No matter how carefully a church hires, there is always a risk of hiring someone who fails to meet the job expectations. Handling such situations are difficult. When should a person be dismissed? What other alternatives are there?

There are certainly cases where the churches should be different from the business world in how they treat their employees. The bottom line (dollars) is the ultimate key indicator in a for-profit business. The purposes of the church (evangelism, edification, education, exaltation) should drive its decisions. I am not making an appeal here for tolerance of insubordination or failure to comply with doctrinal, ethical, and legal expectations. But there appear to be some extenuating cases where dismissal may not be the way to go.

Some examples:

1. *Inherited team members.* If a staff member has served faithfully for many years under previous leadership, that should be recognized and affirmed. Some are simply not hirable elsewhere or so close to retirement it is unreasonable to ask them to move. I believe that under the principle of "with responsibility must come corresponding authority," senior pastors should be given the right to dismiss any staff they deem necessary. However, that does not imply that senior pastors should summarily remove all staff. The mere fact that they can usually provides all the leverage necessary to bring about change.

2. *Wounded team members.* Some staff are giving 100 percent of what they have. For various reasons (health, competency, personality, family), they simply cannot perform at the level the leader would hope. Is it right to fire them for things they cannot correct or improve? The church should not be known for shooting its wounded.

3. *Outgrown team members.* They may have been effective when the church was small. But as it grows, they are simply in over their heads. What they do is not bad; it's just not enough anymore.

4. *Hiring mistakes you are responsible for.* Loyalty is a two-way street. When senior pastors have uprooted someone and brought him to the area, they have an ethical responsibility to make it work if at all possible.

5. *People who are quite capable but not a fit for the new team.* These are relatively easy because they usually sense the new reality and will work with the senior pastor to move on for their own sake and that of the church.

6. *Staff members who want to do too much.* It's ironic how, upon analysis, team members who will not do what they are asked to do and those who constantly are getting into matters they were not asked to, reflect a similar challenge. The bottom line is they don't do what they are supposed to do. Both want to write their own job description. Both tend to diminish the effectiveness of the overall team. Both are in essence attempting to be their own boss.

Many books on leadership will say the organization must get rid of these people. In fact, some of the nationally known type-A leaders have become well known for the revolving door. It is hard to argue with their records of corporate success. Having less than fully competent and excellent performers on the staff may cause some questioning of leadership and consequent lowering of morale. However, it is more destructive to morale when a steady stream of people are pushed out the door for performance they really cannot improve significantly or because the one who hired them miscalculated. Instead, explore options other than dismissal or living with the unacceptable status quo:

Option A — Try to discern where the person can serve effectively. A generally accepted rule of management is that you never demote a person. If they cannot function at the same level or higher, they should go. The local church, however, is a service industry (or more accurately a "servant industry"). What constitutes demotion for a servant? The founder of the church said, "He that will be great must be servant of all."

As a declining church begins to breathe new life, the needs will grow. All team members will be asked to reevaluate their capabilities and role in light of the new realities. Every time there is a staff change, the leader has a valuable opportunity to realign responsibilities for everyone including himself.

This is not the same as marginalizing a person. It is certainly not the same as promoting the problem employee (*never* do that). It is, instead, having the courage to say to a person, "You simply are not capable of taking the next steps here." Perhaps another person can be brought in alongside of them to compensate for their weaknesses.

Option B — Reward them according to what they are capable of doing. It is unfair to the performing team members if everyone is rewarded the same. So, in this scenario, the leader does not reprimand the underperforming team member but rather allows the staff member to transition from full-time to a part-time status. The church is not hurt, for the person still receives value in accordance with the contribution. Also the person is not embarrassed publicly (assuming the staff salaries are not published). If such team members simply cannot live on what they make and are capable of doing better somewhere else, they should do that.

With this option the funds that might have been allocated for a person who was performing with greater cooperation and expertise can be set aside for another part-time person to come alongside of them and care for the areas they are either incapable of or unwilling to accept. Each resignation provides a valuable opportunity to realign the existing staff team. In fact, I cannot recall a resignation during the past 23 years that did not ultimately allow the church a golden opportunity to move to the next level of growth and ministry. Longevity has obvious advantages, but resignations need not be feared. The wise turnaround leader will always be thinking, "What if a vacancy should come open?"

Option C — Assist under-performing team members to find a place better suited for their abilities and interests. This is a last resort, but a loving one. They may believe that the first two options are unacceptable. They may believe that you have inaccurately assessed their contribution and abilities. They may think that they should have more responsibility and a greater part in key decision making. They might feel under-rewarded for what they do, yet unable to find another position.

You have openly interacted regarding the variance between your perception as senior pastor/team leader and theirs. There is no resolution. At that point the reasonable and loving thing to do is to assure them that you will help transition them into a place where they will be happier. At this point you work together. You tell them that during the next 90 days you will pray with them about their new place of employment. They should begin immediately to seek out where they can begin the next chapter of their life. You would like to be one of their best references, but they will need to help you by maintaining a high level of character. Assure them you wish for the parting to be a celebration of what they have done for the church.

Tell them that not only will you hold them accountable for their own behavior during this time of transition, but for the behavior of those closest to them. There is no need for this to end in an unpleasant manner. By working together to seek the next steps in their life, you are doing something a business would seldom consider. Assuming they cooperate, the church will want to be generous in severance considerations.

There are often options other than the three sets outlined above. Your task is first to carefully assess the situation. Next, brainstorm to come up with a list of feasible options. Then weigh the options, carefully considering the implications of each. Finally, select the best option for all concerned.

Leaders of turnaround teams are making choices every day. No one will make all the right choices. However, when it comes to these four areas— the congregation, lay leadership, governing board, and paid staff—turnaround leaders need wisdom for an extremely high batting average.

CHAPTER 8

Coaching Helps: Choices

By Daniel Harkavy

Firing people, helping people to leave your church, picking board members, determining new roles and expectations for volunteer team members. This sounds like gut-wrenching stuff! I would assume that very few of you were trained in seminary to do any of these duties. And no leader is ever truly excited about these duties, but they are required in order to successfully lead turnaround.

Chapter 7 really affirms why the first three chapters of the book are so critical. Can you imagine making any of the above decisions without convictions, commitment, and courage? As a business coach, I can tell you that the majority of the executives who struggle with making the tough calls struggle because they lack the heart. They do not have the convictions to drive the execution; as a result, they never reach levels of greatness in their organizations.

There are others who have all of the heart but they lack clarity. They have no road map and live life in the reactive zone. For them, decision making is too risky, so they often will avoid making choices, thinking this will allow them to avoid conflict or failure. The clarity comes when we have spent the time thinking, praying, planning, processing, and gathering wise counsel. I truly believe that we can all improve our decision-making ability and become better at making choices.

Great choices happen as a result of great thinking. In John Maxwell's book *Thinking for a Change*, he lays out the following process for thinking and changing your life:

1. Changing your thinking changes your beliefs.

2. Changing your beliefs changes your expectations.

3. Changing your expectations changes your attitude.

4. Changing your attitude changes your behavior.

5. Changing your behavior changes your performance.

6. Changing your performance changes your life.

What I observed when reading this is that my choices fall into step 5, changing my behavior changes my performance. My behavior stems from a series of smaller decisions, that when added together, influence how I perform as a leader. Many leaders struggle making even the smallest of decisions because they lack the three essential C's: conviction, commitment, and courage.

Needs for Decision Making

Different people need different data and time frames to make choices. To help, we use behavioral assessments in our coaching organizations known as the DISC language (dominance, influence/inducement, steadiness, and compliance). God has created each of us with different timers and processors. Knowing that each of us processes differently, it is beneficial to know the behavioral style of a leader or potential leader. This is the insight that DISC offers. This insight has helped many understand what type of an environment best allows them to operate, lead, and make choices.

The DISC language is an observable, universal language for behavioral characteristics. Once you learn it, you can understand how to best communicate and influence people in any culture. It is a neutral language.

It is a tool and skill that once mastered will enable you to take your influence and leadership to higher levels by knowing your natural behaviors and adapting them to the natural behavior of others.

DISC is a measurement of behavior and emotions. It is **not** any of the following:

♦ A personality test

- A measurement of intelligence

- A measurement of skills and experiences

- A measurement of education and training

William Moulton Marston was the major developer of the DISC language. In 1928 he wrote *The Emotions of Normal People* in which he outlined these quadrants:

Dominance   (D)

Influence/Inducement   (I)

Steadiness   (S)

Compliance   (C)

D-Dominance

- Emphasizes shaping the environment by overcoming opposition and challenges

- *Tendencies:* getting immediate results, taking action, accepting challenges, making quick decisions

- *Motivations*: challenge, power and authority, direct answers, opportunities for individual accomplishments, freedom from direct control, new and varied activities

- *Fears*: loss of control in their environment; being taken advantage of

- *Visible qualities*: self-confidence, decisiveness, and risk taking

- *Limitations*: lack of concern for others, impatience, moving forward without considering outcomes

Descriptors of a "D"

- Ambitious

- Forceful

- Decisive

♦ Direct

♦ Independent

♦ Challenging

I-influence

♦ Emphasizes shaping the environment by persuading and influencing others

♦ *Tendencies*: involvement with people, making a favorable impression, enthusiasm, entertaining, group participation

♦ *Motivations*: social recognition, group activities, relationships,freedom of expression, freedom from control and detail

♦ *Fears*: social rejection, disapproval, loss of influence

♦ *Visible qualities*: enthusiasm, charm, sociability, persuasiveness,expression of emotion

♦ *Limitations*: impulsiveness, disorganization, and lack of follow-through

Descriptors of an "I"

♦ Expressive

♦ Enthusiastic

♦ Friendly

♦ Demonstrative

♦ Talkative

♦ Stimulating

S-Steadiness

♦ Emphasizes achieving stability, accomplishing tasks by cooperating with others

♦ *Tendencies*: calm, patient, loyal, good listeners

- *Motivations*: infrequent change, stability, sincere appreciation, cooperation, using traditional methods

- *Fears*: loss of stability, the unknown, change, unpredictability

- *Visible qualities*: patience, a team player, stability, methodical approach, calm, easy-going nature, concern for the group

- *Limitations*: overly willing to give, putting their needs last, resistance to positive change

Descriptors of an "S"

- Methodical

- Systematic

- Reliable

- Steady

- Relaxed

- Modest

C-Compliance

- Emphasizes working within circumstances to ensure quality and accuracy

- *Tendencies*: attention to standards and details, analytical thinking, accuracy, diplomacy, and indirect approaches to conflict

- *Motivations*: clearly defined performance expectations, quality and accuracy being valued, reserved and businesslike atmosphere, and articulated standards

- *Fears*: criticism of their work, slipshod methods, situations emotionally out of control

- *Visible qualities*: behavior that is cautious, precise, diplomatic, restrained, perfectionistic, and factual

- *Limitations*: overly critical of self and others, indecision because of desire to collect and analyze data, creativity hampered by a need to follow rules

Descriptors of a "C"

- Analytical

- Contemplative

- Conservative

- Exacting

- Careful

- Deliberative

I share the DiSC language here because I think we can make better choices if we understand how we are wired. We can also coach our teammates so they make the best decisions if we know how to best communicate with them. I have been a student of this language for more than a decade, and it has greatly enhanced how I go about making decisions and, more important, how I help others to make better choices.

The bottom line here is that different people need varying degrees of data, input, and time before they can choose or make a decision. Skilled coaches know how to communicate with all behavioral combinations so that they are most effective when making decisions and when helping others do the same. (This is the same quality needed in leaders: they must understand those they lead.)

Our assistant coaching team members play a huge role in the success of our organization. The majority of them are high ISD combinations. Their primary role is to facilitate and manage the process of the coaching relationship between the coach and the client. Our coaches work with clients on annual contracts and have biweekly phone calls with their clients. Some of our coaches work with over 70 executives and professionals. Each assistant coach supports up to three coaches, so as I am sure you can imagine, they spend a great amount of time interacting with a large number of our clients. Perhaps you can see why a high ISD combination is good for an assistant.

Time Management

This is the biggest area of challenge for most of us when it comes to choices. For some reason we do not understand that for every action, there is a reaction. Every time we say yes to one thing, we are saying no to another. The key is to know what you are saying no to when you say yes—to count the cost of the yes before committing. Life Planning and Ministry planning will enable you to make much better choices with your time. How you choose to invest your time will have the single greatest impact on how you lead turnaround in your church. Are your days filled with your desired amount of prayer, Word studying, planning, preaching, discipling, and coaching? It not, work your way through the Core4 and experience real clarity with how you choose to invest your life.

How we invest our time will also determine what type of team we will build. How we invest our time will also determine what type of life we will live, what type of impact we will have, and what type of difference we will make. Our lives depend on how we go about making the many little choices that come our way each day.

THE SITUATION

Mark Simmons came to us as an executive pastor of a fairly large church here in Oregon. He really wanted to grow in two main areas: priority management and leadership. After going through the first three steps in the Core4 process, we embarked on the fourth step, Priority Management. Mark's days were filled with appointments, meetings, and interruptions. Saying he was frustrated would be an understatement. He worked long hours and was struggling with burnout. He was responsible for a number of different ministries, some of which he did not believe in. Several such ministries began as a result of a member coming to him with a passion of their own, challenging him to support their ministry. Many of them pulled the "God card" telling him that they had been shown a vision or had been told to start ministry XYZ. Not wanting to get in the way of God's plans, he submitted and gave them his stamp of approval. In addition, his assistant would schedule anyone when they wanted to see him if the time was open. Mark could not really account for his time. Due to his lack of boundaries and numerous direct reports, he had no ON Time and therefore felt as if he was failing in his position. He had to stay late just to stay current with his IN Time duties.

THE ACTION PLANS

ACTION PLAN ONE: The first action plan given to Mark was for him to Time Track for a full week. His coach needed to see how he was investing his time in 15-minute increments from the beginning to the end of his workday. For five days straight, he jotted down in 15 minute blocks whom he spoke to and why, what he read and why, and where he went and why. He said this was one of the most painful exercises he had ever been through, even harder than creating his Life Plan.

What he and his coach gleaned from this was that there was no rhythm to his day, no predictable pattern that he or his team could count on. We also gleaned that he spent a big part of his day doing things that he could delegate to others on his team. After reviewing this, he felt a new level of hope knowing that we now knew exactly what we needed to work on and change in order for him to have more impact in his position as a church leader.

ACTION PLAN TWO: His next step was to create his Perfect Week. This is a blank one-week calendar that he was to build around his most important Life Plan activities and Ministry Plan disciplines. He was asked by his coach to create his ideal week, a week that would enable him to be who he desired to be. The biggest change that he mapped out was that he changed his morning hours from IN to ON Time. He made no more appointments in the morning. He also identified when he wanted to be home to participate in his important family activities.

ACTION PLAN THREE: Next, he sat down with his team and shared his Perfect Week with them. He solicited their buy-in and support to make this happen. His assistant was the key to this step being successful. She really needed to know how this would enable him to be a better leader and how it would make her job easier as well.

ACTION PLAN FOUR: Then he prayerfully chose which commitments were in line with his vision and plan. This meant measuring each of his current ministries up against his and the church's overall vision to make sure they fit. This assessment pinpointed four that were not in line with where his church was headed. He then scheduled meetings with the appropriate ministry leaders and advocates to inform them of his decision regarding the future of some of the church's ministries.

ACTION PLAN FIVE: Mark then matched his real life schedule to his Perfect Week schedule (see Figure 8-a for a sample). He cancelled or rescheduled all morning commitments. Also, he and his assistant kept a copy of his Perfect Week laminated on their desks. The goal was to get to a 60 percent success rate within 30 days.

Sample Perfect Week Time Blocking Schedule

Time	Monday	Tuesday	Wednesday	Thursday	Friday	Saturday	Sunday
6:00		✳ Get Up					
6:30		✗ Quiet Time		❖ Men's Group	✗ Quiet Time		
7:00	✳ Get Up	✳ Get Ready for Work			✳ Get Ready for Work	✳ Get Up	✳ Get Up
7:30	✗ Quiet Time (any time)	❖ Plan time	❖	✦ Talk/transition	❖ Plan time	✗ Quiet Time (any time)	✗ Quiet Time (any time)
8:00	✳		❖ Personal Growth Time	✗ Quiet Time	❖		❖ Sermon Review
8:30		❖ Sermon (CRAFT)		❖ Plan time		▼	Prayer Time
9:00				❖			✝ AM Service
9:30		❖	❖				
10:00		Wednesday Prep	Wednesday Prep	Sermon (CRAFT)	Sermon (CRAFT)		✦ Counsel/Greeting
10:30							✝ AM Service
11:00							
11:30		❖ Prospecting				Family	✦ Counsel/Greeting
Noon			❖ Prospecting				▼
12:30		▼ Contacts/Lunch					Lunch/ Meeting
1:00		✦	✦	✦ Prayer Time With Ministerial Association	✦		
1:30							
2:00		Weekly Staff Meeting	Meetings/Mail/ Maintenance		Meetings/Mail/ Maintenance		▼
2:30				✦ Meetings/Mail/ Maintenance			
3:00							
3:30							Family
4:00	▼	✳				❖	
4:30	Family Time	Bend Athletic				Prayer & Prep	
5:00							
5:30							
6:00	▼		✦ Café	▼		✦ Greeting	❖
6:30	Family Devotions		✦ Greeting			✝ Saturday Night Services	FLOCK GROUP
7:00	▼	✦ Evening Meetings	✝ Wednesday Night Services	Family Devotions		✦ Greeting	
7:30						▼	▼
8:00							
8:30		▼					
9:00			▼				
9:30	▼	Prayer/Devotions with Linda					
10:00	✳	Bedtime					

✗ Quiet Time	✳ Personal/Time Off	❖ 4 P's	✝ Church Services
▼ Family Time	✳ Exercise	✦ 3 M's	

FIGURE 8-A

The Results

Mark was our first pastoral client. He is an absolute raving fan and here is why.

Mark completed an impressive Life Plan. Doing this gave him real insight and direction with how he wanted to live out his days. It gave him power and clarity to make the right choices in the areas of his life that were most important to him. He created his Ministry Vision and Plan. This gave him clarity on the opportunities that God was calling him and the church to seize. This also gave him the heart and conviction to make the tough choices that were good for the body over the long haul. He then created his Perfect Week, giving him (and his assistant) clarity on how to be the best steward of his time. There were no more morning phone calls or meetings; they were all scheduled from noon on. This freed him up to focus on teaching and study during his best hours of the day, the morning. The success he experienced with bringing projects to completion was huge due to the choices he made with his time.

Mark described his experience:

> I served as Daniel's first pastor client to see how the Building Champions model would work for people in a ministry context. I found our coaching time to be personally transforming on a number of fronts. I used the life planning exercise to learn more about what truly created meaningful investments in the lives of my family members. The goals I set gave me tangible ways to express love in my relationships. It also helped me to become much more focused in my work and to create space in my schedule for long-term planning and thinking. I became a more balanced person, while also succeeding more at work through greater focus. It was great!

Vision, convictions, courage, counsel, and planning, with the Holy Spirit, give you what you need to make great choices.

Hiring

Selecting the right people for your team is one of the most critical functions of leadership. You can be a fantastic leader, but with a team of the wrong people, your results will be mediocre at best. On the other hand, if you have a team of the best and most sold-out players, great things will happen with very little effort from you. We coach our clients through the following process when hiring:

1. The Task List. List the primary functions the individual will be responsible for. These are functions that are being done in a less than excellent manner by another team member or functions that are not being done today but need to be done in order for the team to turn around and succeed.

2. The Profile. What type of person would be best for this position? List the skills, experiences, and gifts someone should possess in order to succeed in this role.

3. The Position Description. This is the road map for success for this person in his or her position. It should state what their primary role is, what success looks like, what they will be accountable and responsible for, to whom they will report, and how they will be compensated for their work.

4. The Target List. Whom do you know who fits the bill or who may know somebody who does? List the names and begin praying over them.

5. The Training Plan and Schedule. Look at the Task List and create the training plan and schedule for each of the tasks this person will be responsible for. Write down how and when this person will be trained and by whom.

6. Relationships are key for recruiting. Start building relationships with those you think might grow and flourish if they were on your team. Share your written vision with them and see if God is calling them to play a role in it.

7. Pay well. Don't be cheap! Pay as much as you can for the best talent.

8. Recruiting is a process. Solicit help from other team members. Who else on your team will assist with making the hiring choice? I strongly encourage multiple interviews by different people to get a full picture of each candidate. Meet with the prospects in their home—with their family, if they have one. Don't sell them; learn about them. God will make it happen if he wants them on your team.

Replacing

There is nothing worse than walking into your office knowing you have the wrong people on the team. If this is not dealt with, your team will develop a form of cancer that will destroy it over time. Do not allow the wrong people to suffer on your team. They know they are not in the right place. They are not happy there, and many live in fear of being found out. For some, it is just a means to an end.

Turnaround requires more of its team. It requires all of their hearts. The church is why we exist. If you have team members who do not understand the privilege of caring for his bride, they must be helped along. They have been crafted for another work. Help them to find where they can flourish best.

Here are a few coaching tips on this.

1. Once you have completed your ministry Vision and Plan, rehire every team member. Meet with each of them to make sure they not only buy in but see what role they are to play. If they have been crafted for this work, help them to see how. If not, help them identify what work they have been crafted for. We must stop trashing church employees. I have heard many stories of poorly handled dismissals in the church. Take the high road. If someone is not a fit, really pour your all into helping that person find a career where he will flourish.

2. Warn underperforming employees. Written performance reviews are a must. Do them on the hire date and when good or poor performance is noted. Catch them doing things right and hold them accountable for less than acceptable performance—in writing.

Coaching

This topic is covered above. Making the choice to become a proactive coaching leader will require sacrifice from you. The rewards are worth it, but there will be months where they are not felt or seen. Schedule time on a regular basis—biweekly or monthly—to coaching your direct reports.

CHAPTER 9

Changes

By Gene Wood

L ast year I had a number of requests to address the topic of "Breaking through the 300-400 Ceiling." What was fascinating to me was that the requests came within one week of one another. One was from central Iowa. The other from Seoul, Korea. Ninety-five percent of the approximately 400,000 Protestant churches in the United States average less than 400 in Sunday morning worship attendance. I thought that due to the renowned megachurches in Korea, their situation must be different. I recently spoke in the largest Methodist Church in the world, the Kun Nam Church. They claim over 100,000 attenders. Each Sunday they hold five morning services and an evening service in their new auditorium (seating 10,000). I just assumed churches in Korea must have long ago figured out the trick of breaking through the invisible ceilings of growth. But my contact, Rev. Won Young Park, an expert regarding the church landscape there, assured me the 300-400 barrier is as real in Korea as it is in the States.

Note that attendance of 400 constitutes a large church because the average attender only comes to the primary worship service two-thirds of the time. Therefore, if a church averages 400, they actually have 600 regular attenders. The number of people who consider themselves a part of the church is much larger, possibly double that amount. One way to figure that is to look at the Easter attendance figure each year.

Why is it important to grow over 400?

1. Lost people matter to God. I did a presentation in Pennsylvania for some key denominational leaders from one of the larger mainline groups. Throughout the presentation I kept alluding to the driving motivation for growth. I quipped, "Our church thought about changing our letterhead byline to read 'Time is short and hell is hot' but some of our elders didn't feel that was too seeker sensitive." Everybody laughed. Later in a Q & A session, the ranking leader referred back to that comment and with sincerity said: "Gene, you raised an interesting theological issue. I'm not sure how many of our pastors would agree with that. So what can we do?" I thanked him for his honesty but went on to say, "I'm really not sure what can be done if those fundamental convictions are not present."

    Ultimately growth is not about numbers; it is first and primarily about obedience to a great mandate. Jesus came to seek and save the lost. He sends us "as the father sent him" to do what he came to do.

    Leaders who overcome the 400 barrier do so by creating a sense of urgency. Urgency is the energy and motivation for change. The church leader brings urgency by continual focus on the Great Commission (Matthew 28) and the Great Commandment (Matthew 22). For results of such focus, read Luke 3:10 and Acts 2:37.

    a. Some pastor-leaders make the mistake of believing that their team already grasps the basic truths;

    b. assumes that people with facts will arrive at the appropriate conclusions without help; and

    c. thinks that saying something once or twice will get the job done.

2. A disproportionate number of church attenders choose to worship in the five percent of churches that break the 300-400 ceiling. So, if an organization is about touching people, this is important.

3. The church over 400 does have a number of benefits:

    a. *Culture.* As already mentioned, more and more people prefer to worship in a full-service church.

    b. *Convenience.* Larger churches can provide the equivalent of a mall versus a series of isolated specialty shops. This is one-stop shopping.

c. *Attraction*. Larger churches provide options.

d. *Economy*. Larger churches can minister to more people, which produces economy of scale, analogous to megafarms.

e. *Competence*. Larger churches often are able to retain more capable pastoral communicators/teachers.

f. *Depth*. Larger churches can hire specialists for their staff team.

g. *Multiplication*. Larger churches can serve as training centers for other congregations in their vicinity.

As I began to ponder the differences between the larger church (over 400) and churches that live under the ceiling, I concluded there are at least six changes that must occur to break the ceiling. We'll consider them in this chapter. My prayer is that this will be a helpful tool to each of my brethren who are agonizing over how to overcome the obstacles to growth in the location where the Lord has placed them.

Some of the factors mentioned here have been dealt with elsewhere in the book or in my first book, *Leading Turnaround Churches*. However, I hope that pulling all of them together in a single chapter will provide a quick reference to the material so that pastor-leaders can more easily use it with their leadership team.

Change #1: Changing the Role of the Senior Pastor

a. Caregiving Is Not Their Primary Role

The congregation must overcome their expectation that the senior pastor is the one who will care for me. (See chapter 6 of *Leading Turnaround Churches*.) The bottom line is that unmet expectations of the pastor spell disaster for a church. The church simply will not rise above the quality of the perceived relationship between pastor and people.

In a church over 400 the senior pastor cannot be expected to:

♦ Perform all the weddings

♦ Officiate at all funerals

♦ Visit all the sick and hospitalized

♦ Visit all the shut-ins

- Be at every committee and task force meeting

- Prepare more than two teaching/preaching presentations per week (though he might preach multiple services)

- Oversee the worship service

- Be available to walk-in visitors at the office

- Answer the phone at home

- Remember birthdays and anniversaries (except his own!)

- Counsel the members in a formal manner

- Be in the home of each visitor

- Remember the names of everyone who considers themselves a part of the church as well as their extended family.

A church desiring to break the 300-400 ceiling needs to spend a great deal of time talking about the above list. Lay leaders must make the decision to break the barrier with integrity. They cannot look at the list and think, "That is fine for other people—as long as the pastor does all these things for me and my family."

The decision to overcome the 400 barrier is painful for people and pastor. How much pain will your church endure?

b. Spending Time Wisely

Years ago Gordon McDonald gave a presentation on the types of people in the local church; it left a lasting impression on me. He shared that all leaders must deal with four types of people. As I took no notes that day, I do this from memory and apologize if I have inadvertently altered his exact terms. But in essence, this is what he shared:

VDP – Very Difficult (or Draining) People. Most leaders know immediately who these people are. In *Leading Turnaround Churches*, I refer to them as the bucket brigades (pp. 51-53). I also talk about "those who cannot leave" (Chapter 5).

VNP – Very Nice People. They are genuinely kind, complimentary, pleasant to be around, socially adept, and encouraging. But when it comes time to do the work, they cannot be found.

VTP –Very Teachable People. They may have just come to faith in Christ or perhaps been attending church somewhere they did not learn the Scripture. So when they come to your church, they are like a sponge; they cannot get enough teaching and nurturing. They are willing to do whatever they are asked and serve with a joyful attitude.

VIP –Very Important People. These are the engine that drive the church. They, along with VTP, are the 20 percent who do 80 percent of the work and give 80 percent of the contributions.

Looking at the list again:

80/20 Rule

80% VDP – Very **difficult** people
VNP – Very **nice** people

20% VTP – Very **teachable** people
VIP – Very **important** people

FIGURE 9-A

Where do most leaders spend 80 percent of their time? Above the line or below the line? The obvious answer is above the line. We spend time with the handful of difficult people in our church because we wish to placate them and try to keep them happy—a most likely impossible task. We spend time with the VNPs because they make us feel good. They often treat us to dinner at a nice restaurant, pay us warm and flattering compliments, and may offer use of their recreational toys or condo.

The bottom line is that the effectiveness of the church is determined by those below the line. They are the ones funding and doing the ministry. Tragically, when leaders spend most of their time above the line, they only have limited time to invest in those who are making something happen.

This is a formula for disaster.

Leaders determined to build a turnaround team must make a conscious choice to invest 80 percent of their time in those who will move the work forward. Worse yet, when leaders spend a disproportionate amount of time with difficult or flattering people, they are in effect training the new people how to get attention. The message is, be difficult or stroke the ego-needs of the pastor and you will receive attention. Time and attention are ways to reward people. Choose carefully whom and what you reward.

Some will object to this suggestion by arguing that all people are of equal worth to God. This is true. So, I tell our people, "Come on down! There is room beneath the line for everyone."

Change #2: Changing Group Dynamics

Above the 400 level, we cannot view our church as one big happy family. This is another reason many churches choose to stay below this level. In fact, they do not grow for much the same reason that middle-age couples do not have children. They practice a form of birth control. It is seldom spoken out loud. In fact, most people in churches below 300 will deny that they do not really wish to grow larger.

Much good material has been written regarding the group dynamics of a church, but a summary bears repeating here. A local church should be thought of in three ways (see diagram 9b):

a. *Celebration.* Primary goal is worship (no limit to number).

b. *Congregations.* Primary purpose is learning (normally between 20 and 200).

c. *Cells.* Primary purpose is intimacy (less than 15).

a. **Celebration.** The bigger the better.

The Israelites gathered on several occasions for corporate worship. They numbered in the hundreds of thousands. It does not matter. At Grace Church we are unable to meet together except for one time each year on Easter. We rent an indoor sports arena. That morning it is likely regular attenders will not know at least one-half of the attenders. But that does not in any way hinder the purpose of the gathering. We come to celebrate a shared event. We come to meet the

Creator and express our gratitude to him. In many ways those around us are secondary to our function.

I have often shared with our people that "I do not come to church on Sunday morning to have fellowship with them. I come to have a corporate encounter with the God of the universe." Therefore, it does not matter how many are present. In fact, many find the larger the crowd the more meaningful the worship. One reason may be that there is a degree of anonymity in a crowd of people which permits us to momentarily forget ourselves, indeed losing our self-consciousness for a period of time and getting our focus on where it really should be.

b. ***Congregations***. The purpose here is quality holistic learning. Teaching certainly does and should take place from the pulpit. But meaningful interactive and, to some degree, creative life-learning experiences are somewhat limited. The pulpit is often intellectually centered. Information is dispensed. The people listen and on cue rise to leave. Preachers are forced to use a shotgun. They must speak to a wide range of people—with differences in education, age, spiritual maturity, attention spans, and even cultural and ethnic backgrounds.

Congregations, whatever their make-up, offer a group dynamic where teachers can adapt their pedagogical methods to tailor-fit their audience. They can utilize question and answer, role-playing, inductive-discovery methods, group prayer, small group discovery assignments, and other forms of learning.

The teacher in the congregation will also have the freedom to adjust the learning time to accommodate the real needs of the church members as they are uncovered. The teacher in a congregation should know all the members by name. He should soon know at least three things about each person: name, needs, and niche.

c. ***Cells***. The primary purpose here is intimacy. Only in a smaller setting is it safe and appropriate for people to truly open up and share what is happening in their lives. It is here that holistic relations can be developed. (See *Natural Church Development*, Christian Schwarz, published by ChurchSmart Resources.)

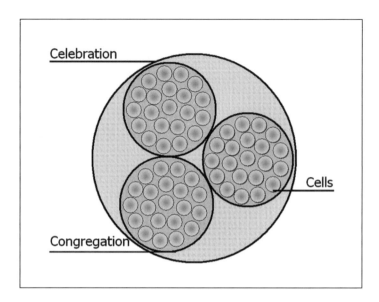

FIGURE 9-B

My goal here is not to repeat at length what has been documented and treated with excellence in many places by church health writers, but rather to stress how critical changing group dynamics is to overcoming the 300-400 ceiling.

A church must stop thinking of itself as one big happy family and understand that congregations and cells will meet the needs which were previously met in one worship service. As many have suggested, this is often sufficient reason alone to begin a second service. Doing so forces a church to deal with the group dynamic changes of growth. The pain can be great. In fact, some who wish to cling to what once was will attempt to attend all the services and even the class meetings for a period of time.

The goal in developing our group life is to move people inward with respect to the concentric circles (see figure 9-d). The innermost circle represents the 20 percent in every church who do 80 percent of the work and give 80 percent of the money.

Those already within the inner circle may complain because more will not join them. They view the lines representing the circles of commitment and involvement as simply "lines on the floor" over which any willing person can easily step to move inward. But those on the outside circumference tend to see these lines as walls, which must be climbed over.

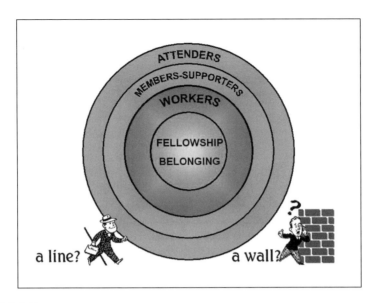

FIGURE 9-D

The single best way to encourage new people to come "in" is to start new congregations and cells, which they can (and are encouraged strongly) to join. These can be in the form of:

♦ New Sunday school classes

♦ New home study groups

♦ Men's groups

♦ Women's groups

♦ Mission teams/short-term trips

♦ Life-stage learning classes (pregnant moms, mothers of preschoolers)

♦ Support groups

♦ Ministry teams (music, grounds and maintenance, prison outreach)

♦ Task forces (building, church school, visioning, etc).

The nature of the group that new people join really does not matter as long as the meetings are to encourage healthy and significant involvement in one another's lives.

Change #3:   Changing the Role of the Governing Board

In the smaller church, the governing board will normally take charge of counting and depositing the offerings, developing the budget, and approving expenditures. All are considered part of their fiduciary responsibility.

In addition, they often consider their role to be that of overseeing day-to-day operations of the facility and paid staff. In the worst case, the board members see themselves as management, and the paid staff as labor. In healthier situations, they would eschew such thinking but nonetheless understand they have a responsibility to keep the church staff accountable for work functions. All significant decisions regarding expenditures and all operational questions should include full board interaction long before it is brought to the public.

In churches under 300 the governing board also tends to consider itself to be a representative one. Each member is placed on the board to represent a subset of the congregation. Just because this is not expressed verbally does not mitigate the reality. Each interest group in the church feels bad if someone is not on the board to lobby its cause. For example:

Board member #1 represents interests of older members over age 60 who wish to maintain the familiar worship styles.

Board member #2 represents the younger adults who are second-generation members and grew up at the church. They know how things have been done but express a desire for some change.

Board member #3 represents the people who have joined during the past 10 years.

Board member #4 represents the women.

Board member #5 represents those who care passionately about foreign missions.

Board member #6 is active with the worship teams.

Board member #7 is actively working with youth.

Churches over 400 move away from such a representative board mindset toward a leadership or governance role.   The board does not come together to make sure each special interest group is heard but rather to ask the question, What is it that God wishes this church to do? They believe that when this question is answered correctly all the groups will benefit and be blessed. Board members are chosen in part on their willingness and ability to think in this new manner.

How should a board function? The answer depends on:

1. The size of the church

2. The tenure and trust earned by the pastor

3. The effectiveness of the pastor in leading

How can a pastor develop trust from the board? What can be done to earn the trust of the board? Let me suggest a number of things worth considering.

1. There is nothing like a good start. An ideal time to establish general working agreements with the board is *before* accepting a call or appointment to a church.

2. Establish a "no surprise" policy.

3. Determine each board agenda ahead of a meeting *with* the lay leader of the board.

4. Be honest in the nominating process. It is tempting in the nominating process to be kind and not voice concerns over nominees who are not competent or not qualified. However, when pastor/leaders acquiesce without comment, there are consequences:

   a. Their implied consent empowers the new (and unqualified) member.

   b. Their silence lessens the respect of others in the process who wonder why the leader did not address the obvious. Someone needs to say, "The emperor is naked."

   c. Once people who are not team players are elected to a governing board post, there will be a long-term problem (usually at least 3-6 years) in which they must be dealt with every month.

   d. The unqualified person then has a say in future nominations and appointments, so the problem escalates.

Apart from the failure to meet the scriptural qualifications, there are other sound reasons to say no to potential board candidates:

a. They are not in agreement with the direction the church is moving. Such candidates view the opportunity to go on the governing board as their chance to alter the direction the church is presently moving.

b. They have an out-of-control spouse. In the church environment couples function best as a team.

Functions of the Board in Churches over 400

A couple of years ago, I was serving as chairman of the board for an international mission organization. We had relocated headquarters and made a few cosmetic changes, but most agreed the time had come to stop putting paint on an old way of doing things and completely overhaul the mission.

I knew that before the mission could change, the board would need to lead the way by reinventing itself. That included not only the scope of board meetings, but an entire attitude of change. We were struggling to know exactly what that entailed. It was at the precise time that I went on my annual study leave. I packed several boxes of books for the week of refueling. About one in the morning I was reading Olan Hendrix's book *Three Dimensions of Leadership* (ChurchSmart Resources) when I came to the final chapter and EUREKA!!! In his chapter titled "Governance/Boardsmanship" (pages 125-146) he spelled out the answers to our questions and problems. I immediately suggested we purchase and mail a copy to each board member. The mission agency is now in the process of moving to this new approach after 55 years of the customary draining bureaucracy and micromanagement.

Hendrix's book introduced me to the John Carver model of governance. I encourage you to pick up his book if you are serious about overhauling your organization's board, executive, and governance systems. It contains an excellent summary of the Carver system.

There is probably more management information available concerning boards than any single management subject. The problem is that almost all the literature deals with the traditional model for board work. To the best of my knowledge only John Carver has devised a totally new model for board work in not-for-profit organizations. He describes this in his excellent book, *Boards That Make a*

Difference. (Hendrix, p. 126)

What I wish to add to the excellent material already available regarding the Carver model is a matter-of-fact series of observations and suggestions as to how the principles of the Carver governance model might be applied to the average church with between 300 and 600 in morning attendance.

Drucker is correct when he observes: "All nonprofit boards have one thing in common. They don't work." For the past 20 years, I have served on all sides of the board table, as chair, CEO/pastor, and board member. Traditional nonprofit boards follow predictable patterns:

1. The boards are larger than they should be. Anytime a board has over 12-14 members, there is an increasing number of passive and silent board members. In fact, the larger the board the smaller the decision-making group. Usually three members end up being the actual decision makers.

2. One or two board members decide they really should function as the CEO of the corporation.

3. Board members begin to manage the staff and oversee the day-to-day functions of workers.

4. Some board members react in the opposite direction and become too passive. For some, serving on a board provides good fellowship and camaraderie. It also provides an excuse for not doing any significant ministry since they are too busy being on the board. And it provides a sense of status and position. Therefore, they do not wish to jeopardize the opportunity to continue serving, making them hesitant to do or say anything that might cause them to be uninvited to serve on the board. Their objective-purpose ceases to be the health of the organization and becomes being liked.

5. Meetings become too long and full of operational minutiae that the board has neither the information nor competency to deal with. There are hours of talk, opinions, argument, and debate with limited action.

6. The board has a steady stream of minority-majority votes, which creates partisan coalitions and creates winners and losers each meeting.

7. When reports are given, they represent the classic "drawing the bullseye around where the arrow is." No one knows exactly what is being

aimed for, so there is never any objective criteria for determining success or failure. The CEO/leader simply finds something that looks positive and declares that is what the organization was attempting to do. One thing you'll seldom see is a long-range chart that shows stagnant growth or decline even if the organization is obviously plateaued or in decline.

8. When board members become aware that little progress is being made toward objectives, they know something should be done but have no clear plan for changing the status quo. They often begin picking at the most convenient targets (pastor, staff, or one another).

9. Surface harmony is perceived to be more important than effectiveness and accomplishment. In churches much emphasis is placed on spiritual quality not being quantifiable.

10. Self-appointed business executives often feel they must take over since nothing is being done. This usually leads to division, not only within the board but within the congregation.

The Need for Change in Governance

Following are twelve indicators that your church needs to consider a new model of governance:

1. You are continually beating your head against the 300-400 ceiling.

2. The staff is unclear about whom they answer to.

3. The senior pastor does not sit in the executive board meetings.

4. The board often attempts to manage the day-to-day functions of the staff.

5. The board is routinely spending time dealing with day-to-day operations issues.

6. There are more than two standing committees.

7. There is not a clear and agreed understanding as to what the future should look like and clear markers for assessing progress toward that future.

8. There are not clear key indicators for determining whether merit raises should be given.

9. Board meetings are more than once a month and last over two hours.

10. The board believes they need to develop the church budget.

11. The board thinks they must be involved in the search for new staff.

12. The church feels it is necessary to look at all salaries.

About 70 to 85 percent of all local churches in North America are plateaued or in decline. This is a problem of epidemic proportions. When a mere few hundred people died worldwide in 2003 during the SARS crisis, the entire world took notice. The continent of Asia was virtually paralyzed. Tourism was halted; the economy took a nosedive. Why cannot the bride of Christ respond to our own crisis with equal commitment to seek a solution? Churches are decaying and dying by the thousands, yet we continue doing what we've always done as if there is no alternative.

Remember: If you always do what you've always done, you'll always get what you've always got. If you like the results you are achieving, then stick with your governance model, means of functioning, and structural procedures. If you long for something new, vital, and effective, it is worth being open to a new way of doing church.

I really do not even wish to present what follows as a new ecclesiology or polity. Those who are congregational in their polity can remain so. Those with hierarchal convictions do not need to toss their ultimate structure. Nor is anyone being asked to set aside biblical convictions. I believe that most any ecclesiology can adopt the suggestions below without compromise to its core values.

Let's simply think of what is suggested as a practical, logical, common-sense, and growth-permitting approach to church government.

Common-Sense Governance

A. The senior pastor is granted authority by the congregation and governing board to function as the chief executive officer for the church.

Many have decried the label of CEO being attributed to the senior pastor as contradicting the scriptural designations: shepherd, bishop, elder, pastor, and so on. So much has been written on this that we simply cannot allow space here to counter point by point the faulty assumptions and straw men that these writers set up. But permit me to present the case for pastor as CEO in a positive manner:

1. One simply cannot make an airtight case for egalitarian plurality of elders in each local church. The term elder does occur in the singular. And when the plural is used, it certainly does not imply that there was more than one elder in each local assembly. To begin with, churches were largely house churches, and when they speak of the "elders" in Ephesus, there was obviously a need for multiple elders. We too quickly extract the first-century reality and impose it on our contemporary larger-church context.

2. The Scriptures do refer to the elder as an overseer (1 Timothy 3:1; Titus 1:7). The elders are also instructed to rule over the flock (1 Timothy 3:4-5; 5:17; Hebrews 13:7). Certainly this is not the primary emphasis of pastoral ministry. In fact the leader is to

    a. protect the flock (Acts 20:29-30),

    b. guard the truth (Titus 1:9),

    c. feed the flock (1 Peter 5:2),

    d. be an example (1 Peter 5:3), and

    e. equip the flock for the work (Ephesians 4:11-12).

    My experience has taught me that when pastors focus on the above, the flock quite readily permits them to rule and lead.

3. The word *lead* means something. I was invited to do a Leading Turnaround Churches seminar a couple of years ago for a small denomination that prides itself on being radical egalitarians. Every member of the church is supposed to have equal voice and vote in determining even the smallest decision. As you might predict, the average congregation is very small. After repeated attempts to reason with some of their leaders as to the biblical necessity for their functioning as CEOs and its practical implications, I finally, in exasperation, blurted out, "What does the word lead mean to you?" My question was met with stunned silence.

4. Because we use the expression "CEO" does not mean that we must imbibe the negative qualities too often associated with corporate leadership (power, status, money, corruption, manipulation, etc.). The initials simply stand for:

   a. "Chief"—refers to "great influence." It can also imply great value or power, but that does not need to be inferred in this case. The chief shepherd was one of great humility.

   b. "Executive"—"relating to or carrying into effect." Whatever plans, direction, values, purposes, or visions are determined by the governing board, this person has the responsibility to see that successful execution of all of these are accomplished.

   c. "Officer"—"one who holds an office of trust." With responsibility must go corresponding authority.

   Let's break it down. When pastors are granted the position of CEO, they are recognized and granted by the congregation and board a position of great trust. Along with that trust, they are granted influence in order to implement daily functions that will achieve the fulfillment of the values, purposes, and visions of the church.

   The bottom line is, why waste money hiring pastors if you cannot and will not trust them to lead in the accomplishment of the church's objectives and goals? Most of the world agrees with the premise that everything rises and falls on leadership—except for some power brokers in declining religious congregations. The results speak for themselves.

   The title of this book is **Leading** *Turnaround Teams*. Effective teams recognize the need for clearly defined leadership. We cannot allow the corruption and abuse of power in some cases to cause us to throw the baby out with the bathwater. A church must seek good leaders, not deny the need for one.

B. The governing board assumes responsibility for establishing policy.

   Most church boards are involved in far too much micromanagement. There may be a number of reasons for this:

1. Some board members find service on the board to be the most significant thing in their life. It becomes a place of influence and power (which they may not have elsewhere). Or board meetings can be a

primary source of socialization. Therefore, the more often the board meets and the longer the meetings, the greater the opportunity for interaction. Larry Osborne in his book *The Unity Factor* recommends boards get together more often, but goes on to say time should be set aside monthly for social interaction and devotional growth. This may be good advice. In this manner the holistic needs of lay leadership can be met in a healthy way that does not confuse the work of governance. Perhaps each board could consider appointing a social chairman to ensure that fellowship and relationship building are addressed.

2. There may be lack of clear definition of what a board should be doing. I am recommending that a church be pastor (staff) directed and board protected.

3. One or two board members (sometimes families) may see themselves as the administrator or "church boss." Such people assume that every operational decision should officially or unofficially be passed by them. This is why many pastors discover the one who first greets them when they come to candidate and is instrumental in their call to the church may be the first one to become unhappy with them when they arrive. These board members expect to be consulted on any significant (a term they reserve the right to define) decisions. When they are not singled out for input, they feel slighted, demeaned, and fearful of what will result. Serving on the board ensures that they can surface anything which may not have been run by them and demand explanation.

Blessed is the pastor who finds lay leaders who have functioned with excellence in the interim period between pastors but are ready to relinquish that role. When we arrived in Lewistown, Pennsylvania, the church had been without a senior pastor for almost four years. During that period of time, they had experienced a serious split, and, in fact, the very existence of the church was at risk. A wonderful man, Earl Buchanan, had been instrumental in holding the ministry together during that period and was the board chair. I was 29 years old and fresh out of seminary. I viewed Mr. Buchanan with great esteem.

When I had been there just a few months, I decided the time might be right for us to gather our leadership team together for what would be my first "annual ownership meeting." I stopped by to visit Earl. He was out in the garden doing some weeding. I squatted down next to him and hesitatingly shared my plan to gather a cross-section of leaders for a weekend and encourage them to help set the direction and priorities for our congregation.

He listened, asked a few questions, and then looked up over his glasses at me and said, "Why are you asking me? You're the pastor. I'm just a layman. Lead!" Earl's attitude and trust resulted in four years of remarkable growth. May God increase his number.

4. Individual ministry calling may be confused with official board function. Of course, board members will frequently be individuals gifted to teach, exhort, administrate, shepherd, encourage, and lead. That is fine. But none of those things are necessarily what they should be doing as a sitting board.

The Role of a Church Board

If you have read *Leading Turnaround Churches*, you are already familiar with the 95 percent theory. That is, 95 percent of all major problems in a local church boil down to power struggles. One way to diminish these is for the board to clearly define what they will do and what they are going to delegate. I suggest the board limit their functions to the following:

a. Determining the boundaries within which the church may function. This may be pictured as a box (see Figure 9-e).

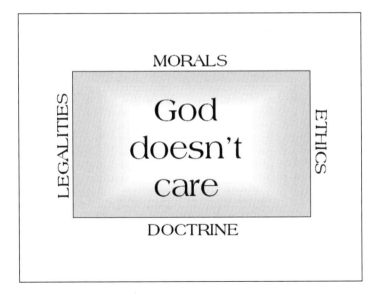

FIGURE 9-E

You may wish to include some of the following when you label your box:

- Doctrine (include ethics, values, morals)

- Philosophy of ministry

- Constitution and By-laws

- Direction (detailed in the church Master Plan and one year goals)

The board retains the right to bring the walls of the defining box in as close as they deem proper or expand the walls of the box to allow for more freedom and wiggle room. But once the walls have been drawn, great thought and prayer should go into adjustments. Any modification should always be made as a full board. No one member of the board has the authority to adjust the box on their own. Adjustments to the box should be done with much discussion and deliberation, and then duly recorded in the board minutes. This box defines the boundaries within which the church pastor and staff can function. They will be held accountable for any action that transcends the boundaries of the box. But they will also be given much freedom to lead within the confines of the box.

b. Determining the master plan (Where we are headed?). What ingredients uniquely define this congregation? What broad descriptive factors will guide our programming, facilities, and staffing? The critical thing here is for each congregation to celebrate the great freedom we have in some matters. Our plan will be as unique as we are. It will likely not be an exact replica of any other church. It is governed by assessing our current reality as a local congregation, taking into consideration our culture, location, demographics, personality, history, economics, and dreams. This is determined at the annual ownership meeting.

c. Affirming and ratifying the one-year goals that will move the church toward its long-range Master Plan. The goals may be recommended by the staff or agreed upon together. Reality suggests that the staff should play a large part in forming the goals since they will be essential for implementing the goals throughout the year.

d. Ensuring that the constitution and bylaws are followed, or making recommendations for amendment of them. Most constitutions require the board to be involved in the sale or purchase of real property.

e. Approving the church budget and making sure that it underwrites the priorities as determined by the master plan and one-year goals. Those closest to the budget lines should probably be given the responsibility to come to the board with their recommendations. Boards make poor committees. Boards, however, should have the privilege of looking over the budget proposal and asking any questions they have—and they should always receive whatever information they request. For a board to function properly, it must have full disclosure.

f. Holding the senior pastor accountable. The board relates to the staff only through the senior pastor. The board is free to ask any question regarding day-to-day operations. The board has the authority to direct the pastor. But this is as a full board, not any individual member. Such directives should take place in a formal manner and should be in the form of adjusting the box, the master plan, or the goals. His annual evaluation should be based upon his ability to effectively implement the plan of the board.

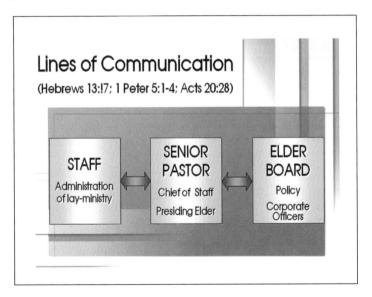

FIGURE 9-F

Finally, here are some questions on changing the role of the governing board:

1. What if our constitution requires the board or even the congregation to vote on staff hiring?

   The obvious answer is to change the constitution. If it simply requires the board to be involved, then the board would have power to delegate that to their senior pastor along with the responsibility for effective oversight and results. Most senior pastors would not wish to bring an executive-level staff member on board, even if they are given unilateral authority, without first being sure their board is comfortable with the hire. To do so is not fair to either the church or to the new staff member. The support of a board can be ensured by open communications of the search and recommendation along with reasons for the choice. A get-acquainted visit with the board is wise before a final decision is made. Perhaps the board will pick up on something the pastor missed in deliberations. Good counsel is always healthy. However, the board will not vote on the staff; it will hold pastors accountable for the choices they make.

2. What might a defining master plan look like?

   The important thing is to avoid making this identical to doctrine and philosophy, which is set mostly by conviction and therefore does not change. The master plan is simply a long-range road map to define how we plan to get to our stated goals. It defines the unique issues of our church. At Grace Church we presently have several distinguishing road markers:

   - We are going to remain at 1515 South Glendora Avenue. This is a significant decision that has a major impact on other decisions. First, we do not hesitate to invest money in tearing down structures on and around our campus. We view ourselves as being right here forever. So, any improvements made are not wasted. Also, we will purchase any adjacent property that becomes available. Don't tell the neighbors, but essentially no price is too high. The decision to buy has already been made.

   - We are committed to multiple worship services. Therefore, we probably will never construct a thousand-seat worship venue. At present, we have four English-speaking services each Sunday. This decision affects staffing, building construction, and the feel of the congregation. We are a community of small congregations, not a megachurch.

- We wish to be a Sunday school church. Most small group life will focus on our campus on Sundays. Among many other things, this drives construction and parking needs. We attempt to keep people on our campus during peak hours for a longer period of time. We must have significant amounts of property for the size of congregation we are. We also must continually build more classrooms. We are presently completing a three-story building for educational and fellowship purposes.

- We will view an average of 2,000 Sunday worshippers as our optimum attendance figure. Beyond that, we will continue to achieve our purposes through either church planting or satellite locations. This means we will be open to purchasing satellite facilities as they become available (we already have one in a city ten miles away).

The purpose in sharing the above is not to suggest a model for any other congregation to mimic. It is a model for no one. The purpose is to help you begin thinking what distinctives might define and steer your church.

3. Do committees have a place in this new paradigm?

No. Committees, no. Task forces, yes. Task forces may be defined as follows:

a. They never take minutes.

b. They are appointed by the staff or governing board.

c. They are given clear budget restrictions (when it's necessary to spend money at all).

d. They report to whomever appoints them.

e. They are put in motion with a mandate to fulfill their task ASAP, then disband immediately.

f. They are disbanded by whomever appoints them.

4. What if pastors do not work within the box?

   Make absolutely clear to them what the box is. If they fail due to misunderstanding, work harder at communication. If they fail due to incompetence, take steps to equip them. If they fail due to insubordination or open doctrinal or philosophical differences, the relationship must be terminated.

5. What if the pastor and the staff team are unable to achieve the goals?

   First, the board should make sure the goals set are realistic. The pastor and team should be included (and in fact may drive) the setting of goals to make sure they are realistic. Failure to achieve goals should not be cause for dismissal. Failure to have clear direction and a plan for achieving progress toward those goals should, however, result in not only the resignation of the pastor but the entire board. A congregation deserves to have leaders who are constantly making efforts toward a preferable future. That is what leadership is all about: taking us from where we are to where we should be.

Change #4: Changing the Role of the Congregation

This may be the most difficult dynamic for a leader who wishes to move his congregation beyond the 400 plateau. Leaders can change themselves. They can work with a dedicated and committed group of leaders to bring change to the board over time. Group dynamics can be changed because the value of small groups is readily proved once they are implemented. But changing the mindset of a congregation that has been in existence for more than two decades is a monumental undertaking. Ninety-five percent of all congregations in the United States, as of this date, have been unwilling to make the change. But it is essential that they begin to view their roles, function, and participation in body life differently if they wish to enjoy all the good things that can come to a healthy growing larger church.

The core issue for some is control. I have attempted to address this at length in *Leading Turnaround Churches*. There I set forth the 95 percent theory, that is, 95 percent of all major conflicts in a church can be boiled down to power struggles. Those issues must be hit head-on, and the officially elected leadership of the church must win this battle.

But there is another difficult challenge. That is to reeducate the majority of churches in America regarding what "congregational government" means. In fact, I am discovering around the world that this reeducation must occur wherever the Western influence has been felt.

Congregationalism Today

Basically, congregationalism is rooted in the New Testament notion of the priesthood of all believers (1 Peter 2:5-9; Revelation 1:6; 5:10; 1 Timothy 2:5; 1 Corinthians 12; Romans 12). Each child of God has the same privilege of going directly to God in prayer, of seeking wisdom and counsel from the Bible, and of following the guidance of the Holy Spirit who lives within. Likewise, each believer has an equal responsibility to speak and follow the dictates of their conscience, as they will give an account to their Lord on judgment day. Some refer to these matters in terms of the "soul liberty" of the believer. In this discussion, they will point out that each believer is given at least one spiritual gift for the building up of the body. Thus, each has responsibility to serve according to the gift given.

Many denominations were founded as Europeans fled the home continent and came to America where they would not be governed by the state or hierarchical authorities.

Closely connected to these concepts is the cherished value of the autonomy of the local church. Many believe that the Bible gives the local congregation the authority to

1. sanction church discipline (1 Corinthians 5; Matthew 18),

2. send missionaries (Acts 13)—the right to commission,

3. select and dismiss their leaders (Acts 6; 1 Timothy 3; Titus 1)—the right to ordain, and

4. settle doctrinal disputes (Acts 15).

I agree with the basic principles listed above. My heritage is baptistic. However, the application of these core principles has played havoc with many local churches' ability to function as they grow larger.

These principles certainly do not make an argument for radical egalitarianism or a leaderless organization.

Following are some other considerations on the issue of congregationalism:

1. Unfortunately, the New Testament provides little didactic material regarding local church leadership. It is always preferable to build out practice on didactive-prescriptive texts rather than narrative-descriptive passages. But in practical ecclesiology, we have little choice. We are almost forced to go to descriptive practice of the early church, and one of the many problems is that there we find apostolic leadership. Question number one is whether pastors wish to position themselves as apostles or even apostolic appointees, such as Timothy and Titus.

2. We must be very careful about removing priestly functions from members. As we do so, we also remove their sense of priestly responsibilities—and then we'll wonder why they see no need to serve, give, pray, or witness.

3. We must also be careful about removing the ultimate responsibility of a congregation in an ecclesiological setting that gives no official authority to the denominational leaders. This sets up pastors as little popes.

4. The New Testament is clear regarding the value of order and structure in church life (see 1 Corinthians 14:26, 33, 40—which not incidentally is a passage focused on proper decorum in local church life).

5. The Bible does talk about leadership (1 Corinthians 16:15-18; Hebrews 13:7,17; 1 Peter 5:1-3). Leadership implies —no— *demands* followership.

6. The Bible also seems to teach unity achieved through consensus building (Ephesians 4:3; Colossians 3:11-15; Acts 4:32; 6:5; 15:22). These passages set forth a tone that seems to have governed the congregational life of the early church when they were healthy: "And let the peace of God rule (umpire) in your hearts." "And it seemed good to us . . ."

A Fresh Look at Congregationalism

When all these considerations are given a place in our ecclesiology, I am confident that congregationalism, while it may need to be reengineered in many unhealthy churches, still has much to commend it.

What does a congregation need to vote on? Simply because I buy a ticket does not mean I get to fly the plane. Congregationalism might best be understood as offering the right to veto power, *not* decision-making privileges. The following charts are helpful in thinking this matter through.

It is true that the congregation may retain ultimate authority under Christ (see Figure 9-g):

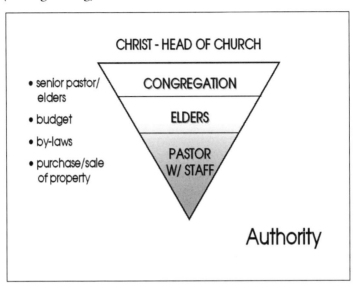

FIGURE 9-G

However, when it comes to function, the triangle might be laid on its side (see Figure 9-h):

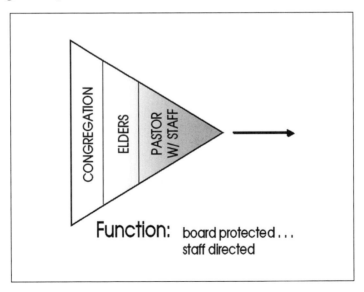

FIGURE 9-H

What are the essentials a church needs to still consider itself to be "congregational"? I, along with a growing number of denominational executives, am suggesting the following as a guideline.

1. The congregation should probably have some say in the call of senior pastors. They should also have final say in their dismissal. If the concepts from the Carver model of board governance are adhered to, this is especially important. Senior pastors will be invested with significant authority to lead the church. Therefore, it is reasonable that they should be accountable to the congregation as a body.

   There is absolutely no need, however, for the congregation to vote on each staff member. Staff is simply an extension of the pastor. This is one reason the group of servant-leaders is most often referred to as the "pastoral staff," not the "church staff."

2. The church should probably have some opportunity to veto an unreasonable budget when it is presented. After all, the membership has responsibility for giving to support the budget. The budget should reflect two things: One, a prioritizing of ministry functions that will accomplish the stated purpose, master plan, and goals of the church. Two, a realistic expectation of charitable giving for the year to support the budget.

   When a congregation is asked to ratify the budget versus actively participate in the development of the same, a great deal of trust must be exercised. Because of this, the board must make two assurances to the congregation. One, the budget will not be overspent without authorization. That is, whatever line items have been voted on at the annual meeting prescribe the cap of spending for that area. Therefore, it is wise to present a simplified budget. The official budget is *not* the place to line item every small possible expenditure. Many congregations do this because a small number of members desire to control the church through the annual business meeting.

   What is budgeted for generously *is* the priority of the church. The budget is a good place to begin trusting the leaders that the church has elected to serve them. A business meeting is the worst possible place to do business. In no place is this truer than when financial matters are being decided.

   In many churches, salaries are actually discussed and often determined in a public business session. Not only is this humiliating to the personnel involved, it is a guaranteed way to create divisions within the church. It is also a sure way to make certain the staff begins to lobby the most vocal and influential spokespersons in the business meetings. This type of behavior does not create effective teams but rather destroys whatever sense of team may develop throughout the year.

A simplified budget will show fewer lines. They are arranged in categories of ministry. Notice that all executive salaries are under one major heading, labeled "administration." Missions has just one figure. How can a church ever achieve unity when the board is forced to explain publicly why one "missionary unit" or "staff member" is given a five percent raise and another only four percent for the coming year? The answer is probably (hopefully) based upon merit, productivity, attitude, and contribution toward the mission, purpose, and goals of the organization. As mentioned elsewhere, any nonprofit that gives across-the-board raises based simply upon tenure is headed for a slow but sure demise. The hard decisions need to be made. But they cannot be made in a public forum where it would not be appropriate and where there isn't enough time to share all the information that goes into these important decisions.

One reasonable way to determine salaries is for senior pastors to recommend salaries for their direct reports. Also, executive staff members make recommendations for those under them. These in turn are brought as a recommendation to the board for consideration of the overall acceptability of the raise for the coming year. The board should then consider the growth or decline of the church, the cost of living index for the year, and financial projections for the coming year. The board could then set a level for overall budget increase (two percent, five percent, seven percent, etc.).

The executive staff that oversees each department of the church should make recommendations (within set guidelines) for their area. These recommendations should include an administrative worksheet wherein itemization of how dollars would be spent is included. This is where it is appropriate to receive justification for the budget request. These are given to the senior pastors for review. In larger churches they may delegate this to an executive pastor (or bookkeeping office). However, I recommend that senior pastors spend at least one day per year reviewing these in detail just to remind themselves how funds are being spent.

Once the staff has presented their recommendations to the senior pastors (or delegate), they review them and make modifications to reflect priorities. The senior pastors then present this to the board. The board has prerogative to modify any portion of the recommendation. Finally, the board presents the final budget proposal to the congregation.

This should be done first in written form. Explain how each budget line will contribute to the ministry priorities of the church. A time for questions and answers should then be offered prior to the business meeting. The first time a church adopts this approach, the primary questions will probably focus on the precise salaries of the pastor and staff. The board will need to determine in advance how they wish to address this.

Interestingly enough, most church bylaws do not actually require full disclosure of salaries. Yet, most church boards assume they do. If yours does not, then that can be stated. At the beginning of this new approach to congregationalism, the spokesperson may need to say: "I know that we have historically broken each detail of our budget down for public dissemination. But that is not necessary, nor is it polite to those who serve us. The overall recommendation for salary increases this year is five percent [or whatever it is]. We're going to ask you to consider this year whether such an increase is reasonable and leave the precise details to the board whom you have elected." The same approach could be taken toward details of missions support.

The congregation still retains the right to veto an excessive budget. But they do so at the macro level, not by becoming involved in minutiae. The first year or two this approach is taken, there may be some unhappy members. But unless your constitution and bylaws actually specify otherwise, most "congregational" churches can use this approach, and the end result will, in time, be much healthier for the church.

When the annual business meeting approaches, it is important to remind people that they had an opportunity to have their questions answered. Explain the process that has led to this budget and call for them to ratify the work of their leaders.

I jokingly share at Leading Turnaround Churches seminars that when I call for the question, it is with an expectation of support—something like: "All those who love the Lord and their church, please vote 'yes.' All those who side with the anti-Christ can vote 'no.'"

The second assurance that must be made when we ask our people to trust us is that leaders will not spend money they do not have! The church, unlike our government, cannot print money. This means the leaders will need to perpetually keep an eye on cash flow. I will sometimes tell our people: "We have a simple concept around here. We don't spend money we don't have. It doesn't matter how large the budget is that you approve. If the giving does not come in, we stop spending. The budget does not tell us what we must spend, only the cap of what we can spend this year."

Each year that goes by in which the people see that their church is fiscally sound, the more trust will be gained.

3. The congregation should have a voice in writing and amending their constitution and bylaws. Each set of bylaws should have some provision wherein the people can call for a special meeting to address issues of major concern. When this provision is removed, the church can no longer call itself congregational.

4. The congregation will want to retain authority to elect and remove their governing board. It is unfair to ask people to follow someone they have no choice in, nor means of dismissing. This, however, does not mean there needs to be a slate of optional names for each governing vacancy. It is more important to find scripturally qualified leaders than to have options. Veto power is the issue here, not a popularity poll. It may be best to present one name for consideration and ask the people to ratify this name after prayerful consideration. Some churches that follow this approach ask that the board be ratified annually. Since the elders and deacons are subject to biblical expectations, it makes sense to ask any who vote no to write next to that vote, on their ballot, the scriptural reason they voted no. This can be immensely helpful to the prospective board members in their personal development.

5. The congregation should probably retain a voice in the sale or purchase of real property. Lending institutions and even governmental departments usually require this. Whenever a line of credit or loan is involved, this too should be affirmed by the church body.

Some Final Considerations on Changing the Role of the Congregation.

The larger a church, the smaller the decision-making body should become. This is a law of inverted proportions. A congregation of a large, growing church will need to select their leadership and let them lead.

This new approach to practical congregationalism does not violate any scriptural principles, nor does it go against most constitutions or bylaws (which could be amended if it does). Most of all, it is a virtual necessity if a church is going to be able to make the adjustments required to allow for significant growth.

1. Larger churches are the new reality.

2. More streamlined systems are necessary.

3. Speed of change increases exponentially.

We now arrive at a classic chicken-and-egg question. Which one comes first: Do we adjust our systems to grow, or does growth force us to adjust our operational systems? I don't know the answer to that, but I do know that cumbersome congregational systems are not conducive to the steady flow (or flood) of changes that must be made in a larger, growing, and outreach-focused church or institution. In fact, we either give up our entrenched systems wherein each member feels a need (or right) to be consulted on every decision, or we will continue to watch as 70 - 85 percent of all our churches plateau or decline.

I stated in *Leading Turnaround Churches* that vitality must begin with the leaders. Here is as good a place as any to begin. Our people must give up the old habits of public bickering, small-church thinking, distrust of leadership, and micromanagement, or churches will continue to be ineffective and die.

Some churches simply cannot understand how fast organizational mechanisms change with growth because they have not experienced it in so long or they stop it when it begins to happen.

Richard Swenson, in his excellent book *Margin*, presented a puzzle to 21 students. Figure 9-1 shows the puzzle and a summary of the student's answers.

```
Puzzle:  If you folded a piece of paper in
half forty times, how thick would the
result be?
```

Answer	Number of Students
Less than one foot	13
Greater than one foot, up to one mile	5
Greater than one mile, up to 2000 miles	2
Greater than 2000 miles	0

FIGURE 9-I

The answer is "Greater than 2000 miles." The first time I read this, I sat at my desk and calculated it by folding a piece of 8 ½" x 11" piece of paper as many times as I could, then measured it with a ruler and did the math. It is indeed very close to 2000 miles. This is an excellent illustration of what happens when a church grows.

If you have multiple children, you understand that each time you brought home a new son or daughter, your workload was not just added to, but it grew exponentially. Your life became forever more complicated and challenging. This is what happens when a church begins to add just 5-10 percent per year to its membership. Forget all the church growth talk of double-digit growth. That is wonderful when it happens, but in turn-around discussions we are just considering what it would be like to see steady growth of any percentage for a number of consecutive years.

Whenever these types of practical discussions begin, someone is sure to point out a healthy growing church that has maintained a rather cumbersome system of multiple boards, committees, and congregational meetings. I know of one in Grand Rapids, Michigan. It is a great church with a great leader, with exceptional growth. But this is a rare exception; in almost all cases the old system simply does not work.

As one who has grown up in a staunch congregational system and has maintained a commitment to the basic tenets of the same, I come to you as one of your own. I am not advocating heirarchialism or a modified form of Episcopalian ecclesiology, but rather maintaining that we must deal with our own man-made applications of deeper convictions. Ask once again, Is what we are doing working? What convictions would I actually be forsaking to take the suggestions above? Why am I unwilling to make the changes? If the latter question is only because of fear, then ask yourself what price you are paying for continuing to function the way you always have.

Ready to make changes? If so, I refer you to Appendix B. There you will find ten helpful and pointed suggestions. Use the appendix as a checklist as you take the next steps.

CHAPTER 10

Coaching Helps: Changes

By Daniel Harkavy

Why do some thrive on change?

Taxes, death, and changes are all unavoidable. What I have observed in some of our most successful business leaders is how they prepare for and embrace change. It is almost hard-wired into their DNA. They are change-aholics. The leader changes, the organization sees the change and they embrace it, the product or service then changes, and we, the consumers, benefit from the improvement. Well, most of the time anyway. In Japan it is called kaizan: continual and never-ending improvement.

I believe that those who thrive on change do so because they see how the process glorifies God how and the outcome affects the team members and customers. They are charged by leading with excellence, and they know excellence is not a final destination but rather a daily battle. Those who are committed to leading with excellence know that they will need to personally grow until they stop leading. They build a culture that embraces change due to their deep convictions about excellence. They know that the opposite of change is stagnation, and that stagnation ultimately leads to erosion and then to failure.

Please, no more change. I am almost comfortable with where we will be next month!

We also work with many leaders who are at the end of their change rope. They have exceeded their change limit. The change tilt light is flashing.

Others are just not wired for change. They prefer an environment of stability and security. The continual changes in the economy, the competition, products, and team members takes its toll on them. As coaches, we are responsible for helping them to embrace and prepare for change, to almost seek it out so that it comes on their terms instead of forcing them to react to it. We see no real difference in our two coaching organizations. Church leaders and business leaders must both embrace change if they want to lead their teams to greater heights. The second word of the title of this book, turnaround, implies change. God willing, you will be used to change the direction of your team and, in so doing, the direction of your church.

Change happens.

This I know: change happens. We cannot escape it. Just look at your church. List every significant change you have seen or been a part of in the last year. In just one year, what do you see? If you're like most pastors, the list is long. You have had changes in direction, staffing, leadership, attendance, facilities, and finances, just to mention a few.

How can leaders improve their change tolerance? The answer lies in the clarity of his vision. As we saw in chapter 4, great leaders see a greater future. This greater reality implies that where we are heading is different than where we are today. We must change things to go from the here and now to there.

Change must happen. Effective teams have no room for prima donnas. If you find yourself or one of your team members continually reminiscing about how it was done before, the red warning light is flashing. Yes, we should look at yesterday's successes and failures and learn from them, but when change is needed, we cannot get stuck on the old ways.

God really sets us up for change in Proverbs 3:5-6. He tells us to trust in him and to lean not on our own understanding but in all our ways acknowledge him and he will make our paths straight. This is very much about change! Think about it. If he did not want us to change, we would not have to trust in him. We could be comfortable with where we are and who we are right now. No change means no faith required. Big changes often require big faith.

Some people change with the direction of the wind.

Some may like change too much. They have not taken the time to really seek out what God has in store for them and their flock, and they change whenever they hear of the newest quick-growth fad. They change after every seminar, workshop and book. They lead by listening to man instead of listening to God. Sure leaders are in need of quiet time with Jesus. They are in need of what I call the "daily vacation." This is that special early morning time when you meet with Jesus, your ultimate counselor, and gain perspective and instruction on how you are to conduct your day. It is not time spent studying for the weekend's message. It is time spent with your Creator with the focus being on him and his plans for you and his church.

I am not bashing those who have been blessed with abundant success in growing their churches and are now teaching others how they did it. I am admonishing those who attend these seminars and immediately begin implementing the new model promoted without assessing how what they have learned meshes with what God has told them to do.

This causes a great deal of strife within a team. The continual starts and stops that come with a visionless leader wear a team down fast. They get tossed to and fro like a ship with no rudder. This is not how you lead turnaround.

Is the 400 number important to you?

Is breaking through the 400 barrier important to you? Read your vision. Do you see 400 plus? If so, why? If not, why not? This must be more than a strategy; it must be in your heart. If the Lord shows you the number, it must be incorporated into your vision-casting meetings, your board meetings, your strategic plan, your one-on-one meetings with your team; it must be about the people and the commandment.

What needs to change in you in order for you to lead the vision God has given to you? What must you learn, how must you develop, who must you spend time with in order to take your leadership skills to the levels that will allow your church to experience the kind of turnaround Gene talks about with a church of 400 or more? More important, what must you stop doing in order to lead your team to turnaround?

In the business world, my associate Todd Duncan teaches that you must clean up before you can clean up. He is saying that we must clean up our messes in order to clean up in cash. In other words, we must rid ourselves of the day-to-day clutter and minutiae in order to really experience all that God has called us to be. I have seen too many leaders fill their calendars with nonleader activities.

Sometimes leaders may not even know why they do these things; They may never have thought about it. In other cases, the following false assumptions may be the cause:

- ◆ "I am a servant leader and therefore must serve my assistant by doing work that may be insulting him."

- ◆ "Nobody here can do it as well as I can, therefore I must do it myself."

- ◆ "If I don't do it, nobody else will get it done, and the church will fail."

- ◆ "Training them will just take too much time; doing it myself is faster."

I become very frustrated when I see great men and women, on whom God has bestowed the gifts and responsibilities of leadership, get stymied by the above erroneous assumptions. Yes, there is only one right way to lead, and it is to serve! But serve in your gift zone. Spend the majority of your time doing what God has called you to do—leading. This may mean many different things to you at different times in your leadership journey. Walt Wiley defines leadership as "leading for the accomplishment of goals for the glory of God and the fulfillment of the followers." The real question is, Are you spending the majority of your time leading others for the greater cause? Are your efforts leading to replication and growth, or are they simply contributing to maintenance? If the latter is your reality, you must spend time identifying what you do best and what God has called you to do.

What happens if you lose sight of the "why"?

In the business world, we see professionals experience burn out when they forget the "why". When money, power, or position become their "why", dissatisfaction and burn out become their realities. When the "why" is answered by something more meaningful, such as people being served, educated, protected, made more efficient and communities being helped, then passion results. We are all in some form of business. Good businesses have products that in some way help people. Bad businesses don't. Your business is the greatest business of all; you are taking care of people's eternal destiny. Your product lasts forever. There is no business like it! Growing God's kingdom and changing people's destiny is your "why". Don't ever lose sight of that.

What really needs to change in order for a team to experience turnaround? The answer is YOU!

In order for the team to change, the leader must change first.

The leader must change in the following areas.

1. **Mindset**: In the business world, the number one cause for business failure is leader failure. We see too many great producers or technicians get promoted to leadership positions without the necessary gifts, skill sets, and training. Corporate America makes the mistake of promoting some of its best producers thinking that they will be great leaders. They don't see the huge difference in skill sets between the producer and the leader and in the end lose great talent. Another mistake is made when great producers think they can do it better than their current leader. They have no real training and maybe too much pride or greed so they try to do it themselves. Following is an example of how this plays out in the business world.

A very hard-working young salesman, Johnny Jones, builds up a great reputation in his territory. His product is well known and very well liked. He works for a company of high repute and receives hours of in depth training and support. With great leadership and coaching, he masters the selling skills required to turn his territory into one of the most profitable in his company. Then he gets a little greedy and thinks he is giving too much to his employer in exchange for them doing very little for him.

Now that he believes he has made it, he decides it is time to break out of the corporate machine to do his own thing. He opens Johnny Jones Widget Sales and begins the exciting journey to entrepreneurial fortune and fame. His first days are filled with discussions with the manufacturers and vendors who will be providing him the products to sell. He reviews the contracts and thinks they are nonnegotiable. In his fervor to get the ball rolling, he signs them without due diligence. Because he is so skilled in sales, he does not see the need to create a business or marketing plan, or a vision, just his calendar, goals, and timelines, which are all production focused.

His reputation is such that he is able to win over some accounts that are willing to give him a try, especially with his discounted prices. He has discounted them of course, to take business from the competition; he knows this is a very common short-term strategy. The orders begin to pile in and with the orders come paperwork, accounting issues, delivery issues, and quality issues; his days become longer than ever before.

His margins are thin due to the discounted pricing, so he cannot afford help unless he borrows to make it happen. Having no solid plan or experience running a company, he is unable to obtain any corporate money and is forced to borrow from his already maxed credit cards and the line of credit on his home. He then makes his first hire. This is his first real management experience, and he hires the candidate with the best personality, someone who is actually very much like him. "This is great" he thinks. "I have found my clone."

Johnny was never really good at the detail work. He is more of a visionary and an influencer, so details were never of real importance. Unfortunately, his assistant, Jimmy is wired the same way he is. Johnny does not take the time to create a position description or a daily task list, so he is really not sure if Jimmy is an asset or a liability. Truthfully, he can't even articulate all that the job entails. His real need is a person with opposite skill sets and experience to help him facilitate the accounting and fulfillment of the sale. The end result is that he has placed the wrong body in a position where detail work is crucial.

Things are still not getting done, so he hires more people and throws more bodies at his problems. With no clear job descriptions, very poor communication due to the volumes of work, no real training and no accountability, Johnny does his best to lead his team. He does not yet understand the importance of profiling and utilizing behavioral assessments to ensure that the right hiring decisions are being made.

You can see how the story unfolds. With his faltering service levels, his accounting errors, and his thin margins, he is unable to compete. Within two years he has to close his doors and file for bankruptcy. A wounded and humbled Johnny now understands the difference between being a great producer and a great leader. With his tail between his legs, he returns to his old corporate position but in a new territory. A tired, beat-up Johnny does not have what it takes to develop a new territory. He soon finds himself unemployed and on mood medications to make it through his day.

A sad and ridiculous story? Sad yes, ridiculous no. Unfortunately, this story is very common in the business world. Businesses fail when technicians run them without understanding leadership and management.

It is no different in the church world.

In my conversations with our pastoral coaches, I have learned that there is a very similar pattern for leaders in the church world. Some of you have been blessed with great preaching skills, others with incredible counseling skills, and some with wonderful musical talent. These gifts have spring-boarded you into positions of leadership within the church. Your years of seminary did not prepare you for the leadership demands you now face. You now know the leadership truth: in order for your church to grow, you must grow as a leader.

The problem is when and how to grow? In the beginning days of your ministry, you probably had time to work on your skills and your knowledge. I have heard some pastors joke that when they started their church, there were ten people there on Sunday morning. If that was your reality when you started, you had an abundance of time.

Then the people came, bringing their hurts, their questions, their needs, and their friends. Your free time became a distant memory, and, with the increases in people, you experienced the increases in responsibility and demands. There comes a point where we all as leaders reach our limits. The church outgrows our leadership.

At this point, you have a decision to make. You can do one of three things:

a. **Ignore**. Ignore the pain and continue to react to the daily needs of the church. This will cause plateau.

b. **Flee**. Allow the burnout to take you out. Raise the white flag and allow a pastor with larger-church experience to take over.

c. **Lead**. Become a student and learn how to reengineer your position and your team. Change how you see yourself, how you conduct your daily activities, and, how you build your leadership team. Ask God to fill you with his Spirit and to give you what you need to step out in faith and grow as a leader.

2. **Prayer**: How much time do you spend communicating with God about his church and his plans for you? Our spiritual lives grow as our prayer lives grow. The better the connection to him, the better the execution for him. I think John 15:5 says it all: "Yes, I am the vine; you are the branches. Those who remain in me, and I in them, will produce much fruit. For apart from me you can do nothing."

3. **Walk**: We are to pray, for sure, but we are also to walk in faith. He opens the doors, but we must have the faith and the courage to walk through them. What doors are being held open for you? What do you have to lose? I want to share a simple game that I play whenever I

have to make a big decision. I call it "worst-case thinking." It goes something like this.

♦ I pray.

♦ I assess the situation.

♦ I evaluate the ramifications of my decision.

♦ I seek out godly counsel.

♦ I ask myself this question: what is the worst-case scenario of my making this decision? If I can deal with the worst case, I step through the door. If not, I take more time or I pass.

4. **Planning**: Planning is more than a skill. It is an exercise. It requires your mind to do some heavy lifting. Planning is greatly enhanced when you elicit help from others who share the vision but have different skill sets.

Planning is the process of assessing reality, identifying objectives, setting strategy, creating action plans, communicating the plans, delegating to the appropriate members, setting expectations, following up, correcting and adjusting, evaluating again, and then celebrating.

Planning is a stewardship issue. Poor planning or no planning can bring us and others ruin and shame. Here are two very important points, planning is a discipline and it is essential for winning teams.

5. **Communicating**: How we say what we say can be more important than what we say. In this advanced, technology-driven culture, time to communicate and build relationships is getting harder to find. As leaders we find our schedules so pressed that finding time to really connect with key members of our team is next to impossible.

There is a solution for this: schedule regular chat times with your team. This can mean bringing lunch in, one-on-one checkups, recreation time, and so on. At Building Champions, I find some of my best communication time to be at lunch. Many of us go to the gym across the street or go for a run during our lunch break. This has been a rich time of communication and relationship building for me. Some play golf, others have weekly Starbucks times.

The key is to ensure that you, as the leader, are connecting with the key people on your team and in your church. The action plan here is to make sure it is a regular part of your week—not just with your elders and congregation members, but with your team members. This is a key to successful turnaround. The team feeds off the vision, convictions, and direction of its leader. Communicating is one of your highest pay-off activities.

There is more to communicating than talking. Talking should only occupy 30 percent of your normal conversation time. Listening, really understanding the meaning behind the words, is the magic ingredient in healthy communication. So few leaders truly understand this.

I know this mistake first-hand; I struggle with it on a regular basis. It is not that I think I know it all or that what I have to say is more important than what my team members have to say. It is a warped perception of what leadership is. In my earlier years of leadership I thought my job was to amaze my team members with timely and insightful instructions and orders that would propel us to unfathomable heights. I owe those poor people an apology.

Active listening shows that we care. Our communication skills improve when we master active listening. It is the ultimate demonstration of caring for another. We love to be heard and understood, to spend time with those who really listen to us.

This is how active listening works:

- ◆ Listen.

- ◆ Write down key points.

- ◆ Nod and agree during the conversation.

Stop and paraphrase what was said to ensure that you comprehend not only what was said but also the heart of the issue.

It sounds simple, doesn't it? Try it with your team, your spouse, your children, and your friends. You will find it to be very difficult in the beginning but very rewarding and fulfilling over time. This one skill can propel your leadership and your team in big ways.

6. **Team Building**: Unity, unity, unity! Unity is the heartbeat of a healthy team. A team consists of different people with varied life experiences, and unique and dynamic gifts, who are called together for

one cause. Without God long-term unity is next to impossible. Healthy teams enjoy co-laboring together. They respect one another. They put the needs of the team and its members ahead of their own needs. They know what is expected of them, and they are trained to perform with excellence. They share the load, they share the victories, and they have fellowship together. For them, they have no job—they have a mission! They own the mission at a heart level and are willing to fight for it. This may sound like a broken record, but this is just one more reason for writing down your vision and sharing it so frequently that it defines your church culture.

Champion teams confront issues. They do not gossip. They follow God's plan for dealing with conflict. They promote open and truthful dialog. They do not fear their leaders; they respect them and care for them. They care enough to confront their leaders when they are out of line. They see this being modeled by their leaders. Champion teams have several leaders. There is not just one leader but many to help shoulder the load. Smart senior leaders will spend a good percentage of their time coaching their leaders so that they are promoting the cause and building the team in accordance to your vision. Great leaders do not control the team members; they control the vision and the values and encourage and equip the other leaders to build the united team culture.

Following are some of the practical ingredients of Champion Team Building.

◆ Hire the right people.

◆ Cast the vision all the time.

◆ Pray with the team daily.

◆ Communicate expectations and roles with clarity.

◆ Be present. An absent leader builds little equity especially during the early days of the team.

◆ Cross train.

◆ Have your team members share their roles, talents, and needs with each other.

◆ Celebrate often and include the team members' families as often as possible.

- Never give negative feedback in public.

- Praise in public often.

- Spend one-on-one time with your team members.

- Have team meetings on a regular basis.

- Study and learn. Create a life-long learning environment.

- Do not tolerate gossip; confront gossipers.

- Be transparent and dependent on the Lord, not the team.

- Practice active listening.

- Create a culture of discipline and accountability.

- When you blow it, apologize and ask for forgiveness.

- Coach your teammates on a regular basis—at least monthly.

- Model self-development and share what you learn. Encourage others to grow as well.

- Pay people as well as you can.

- Don't control the team; you do not own it!

7. **Thinking**: Your thinking affects your actions and your actions affect your team. The best leaders are regular thinkers, habitual thinkers. Thinking is a lost discipline for most leaders. We rarely take the time to sit and think; yet, when we do, the results are fantastic. Great leaders have developed the discipline of thinking. They have a regular time scheduled in their busy lives just to think. This does not include reading or studying; it is just thinking.

Raymond Gleason is the Vice President of Strategy and Learning at Building Champions. His job is to teach us new processes, methods, and tools that will enable us to be more valuable as coaches to our clients. He really hit one out of the park this year when he taught us parallel thinking, using Six Thinking Hats ®. This incredibly powerful tool, created by Edward de Bono, is currently being used to help thousands of leaders worldwide improve how they think. I highly recommend his book, *The Six Thinking Hats*. That book and John Maxwell's book *Thinking for a Change* have really made a difference in how I go about thinking.

John Maxwell told me about a year ago to buy a thinking chair—a leather chair for my home study with an ottoman so I could sit back, put my feet up and think. I did as he suggested and bought two leather chairs. One is by my bookshelf and is for study and reading; the other is by my desk and is for thinking. I don't sit in it unless I am thinking; this chair and my journal are all I need to take my thinking to new heights. I strongly recommend having a thinking place and becoming a regular thinker.

8. **Recruiting**: Hiring the right team members is crucial to leading a team through turnaround. The people you recruit as staff members, elders, and lay leaders will determine the level of turnaround your church will achieve. Remember that recruiting is based on relationship building, and relationships take time. Great people are committed people and will not usually jump ship or commit to a new responsibility overnight. They take their time when making such big decisions. Knowing the facts, as well as the heart of the leader, is required knowledge before they commit.

The following tips will help you improve the quality of your recruiting—and of your recruits.

a. *Create a position description.* What will the person be responsible for? To whom will they report? What are the expectations for this person? How will this person be compensated?

b. *Write out the profile* of the individual you are looking for before you begin the search. What characteristics, gifts, talents, and experiences are you looking for? Writing this out will add clarity. You may be surprised to see that this process causes you to seek out someone with different skills sets than you previously thought important.

c. *Create the target list.* Whom do you know who fits the profile or knows of someone who might fit the profile?

d. *Interview the candidates.* We call the first interview a high-trust interview. In this interview, you want to find out what really makes that candidate tick. Do not sell them on the opportunity. Get to know their heart, their skills, and their dreams. Assess your ability to add value to their lives. Can you see how God will use them and bless them in this position? Or do you want them only for selfish reasons? Will this position harm them over the long haul?

In both of our coaching organizations, we are looking for calling. Are they called to do what we are looking for? This is found out over time and cannot be answered in a simple one-time dialog. Have faith my friends: where God gives us vision, he gives us the resources—and team members are critical resources. My associate Todd Duncan has written a great book called *High-Trust Selling*, which really goes into depth on this process.

e. *Add value.* Look for ways to grow the candidates and add value to their life, even before you offer them a position. If they like journaling, send them thoughts on how to journal and maybe a new journal as a gift. If they like golf, look for a unique golf gift. If they are at a stage of life where they are parenting teenagers and you have already walked in their shoes, send them some dating guidelines you found helpful. You get the picture—get creative and go out of your way to add value to them.

f. *Interview them again.* Include their spouses. Meet with them in one of their settings, maybe their home or office. See how they live and lead. This step is often overlooked and can be very telling. How do they interact with those closest to them? Are they organized or creative? What do you see, and what do you feel? Remember, recruiting is based on relationships and relationships take time, so interview them at least three times.

g. *Have other trusted members of your team interview them.* Their perspectives and insights can be very powerful. Not only this, including them in the hiring decision will help them welcome the new team member with open arms.

"I have a team and I don't know if they are a right fit." If you have inherited a team, or are not sure if you have the right team members, go through the above process and literally reinterview and rehire them. Do they really fit their current position, or would they better perform in a different position on the team? If they don't fit anywhere on your team, help them find their calling and a place where they will fit outside of your church.

9. **Coaching**: Great leaders are great coaches. Some coach unintentionally while others are very intentional. I believe all of us as leaders can

grow our influence and help others reach their full potential if we improve how we coach. The great coach Tom Landry says: "A coach is someone who tells you what you don't want to hear, shows you what you don't want to see, so that you can become what you've always known you could be."

A coach helps others to succeed. Who does not want to do that! What is more fulfilling and significant than being used to help others reach their full potential? My life verse is Colossians 1: 28-29: "Him we preach, warning every man and teaching every man in all wisdom that we may present all men perfect in Christ Jesus. To this end, I also labor, striving to His working which works in me mightily." This says it all. Paul was a coach. He went about warning and teaching so that all people could reach their full potential, being made perfect in Jesus.

For those of you who want to be more intentional in how you coach, here is a very simple coaching process guaranteed to improve how you lead turnaround, one team member at a time.

a. *Pray for the heart of a coach.* Helping others to see what they can become and how they can get there energizes a coach. Colossians 1:28-29 describes the heart of a coach.

b. *Write out your coaching plan.* In what core areas of a team member are you interested? Feel free to use our Core4 model. We have found this to be highly effective with helping people like you improve how they live and how they lead.

c. *Allocate the time to coaching.* Our organization's first coaching session is two hours long and covers life planning. Proverbs 20:5 says "The plans of a man's heart are deep waters, but a man of understanding draws them out." We believe that we must help our team members really define who the Lord has called them to be in all key areas of their life before we can help them lead their teams or improve their organizations. We then move through the other core components to really help the team members gain clarity on the who, how, when, and why aspects of how they lead.

After the first two-hour session, we spend 30 minutes every two weeks with our team members, helping them to make the changes that are congruent with their Core4. Our clients hire us for a minimum of one year and many stay with us for many more. Some of us coach our team members the same way, while others spend one hour per month with their team member instead of using the biweekly model. Both methods work very well, but I suggest meeting biweekly with a newer team member or when the pain involved with turnaround is great.

d *Create the coaching road map.* A key to coaching is gaining clarity on where your team member wants to go and who you, as their leader, sees them becoming. Action plans and accountability have to be at the core of your road map. It is critical that you keep a running log of all action plans committed to by your team members. You must also help them identify the amount of time required for the action plan and the target completion date.

In the best-selling business book *Good to Great* by Jim Collins, he talks about great companies having a "culture of discipline." They include improving and action planning as a part of their daily dialog. This is where you want your team to be. Also, the better you are at completing your own action plans, the better your team will be. They model what they see, so I suggest that you find your coach at once.

e. *Stick to the plan.* In order to really build a coaching culture, you must be 100 percent committed to the plan. If you begin missing your coaching sessions or constantly rescheduling them, your team will know how unimportant their growth is to you. This will lead to coaching suicide. Stick to the plan you create.

Don't build a fence around what you've created. Expand your borders.

We see business professionals reach new heights that are beyond what they envisioned. When organizations outgrow the leaders' vision, the leaders will do one of two things. They will either build a fence around what they have created with the goal of protecting and maintaining it, or they will revise the vision and expand their borders.

When leaders choose to protect and maintain, decline is on the horizon. Such leaders can go into a fear mode instead of a warrior mode. The fear mode comes from their knowing the organization has outgrown their abilities and the value they bring to the team. They do not want to be found out, nor do they have the emotional reserves to take new ground. The last failure rocked them, and they do not think they can afford to take a risk like that again. Growth stops, policies change to protect instead of grow, fear permeates the culture, the prophecy is fulfilled, and business begins its slump. The bottom line is that they lack the faith to risk being transparent or seek out help. They no longer see the value in growing themselves.

On the other hand, warrior leaders realize that the organization outgrew their skills and abilities. They take note of the past failures and learn from them. They upgrade the caliber of their advisors and admit their fears. They obtain help from a coach, read the right books, and redefine who they are and what they will do in order to lead the team into the future. The business continues to grow, services are improved, new products are offered, the team is challenged to grow, and the culture is fun, passionate, and exciting. They see the new vision and feel empowered as a result of their team seeing it as well. This is what we call faith.

Can you see this in the church world?

The decision to overcome the 400 barrier can be painful. That is why writing your vision is mandatory. There will be many days when the pain may feel insurmountable. This is when you pull out the vision document and read it again. We are told to focus on what is good, true, worthy of praise—things of excellence. Our minds should dwell on these things.

The pain could cause you to lose sight of these things and give Satan an opportunity to fill your mind with doubts: "Growing is not what God wants ….You're making bad moves ….You're hurting people to grow the church ….You will fail and they will fire you…. How can any of this please Him?" You have heard these accusations before. Reading your vision document and knowing that God is in the business of giving vision to those he calls will keep you focused on what is good, that is, growing those in your flock—his bride.

CHAPTER 11

Characteristics of Excellent Teams

By Gene Wood

B y now many students of turnaround, and leadership in general, have familiarized themselves with the unique insights of Jim Collins in his latest book, *Good to Great.* In that study, he shares how the task of a leader is to "get the right people on the bus, get the wrong people off the bus, and then get the people on the bus in the right seats." Simple, yet profound.

But who are the right people to have on your leadership team bus? There are at least ten identifiable characteristics of a team that wins.

1. Players on the team are appointed (or somehow selected) based upon their proven commitment, abilities, gift-mix, personality, and willingness to cooperate.

    a. *Commitment*: If candidates do not have commitment to the local church and the task at hand, it doesn't matter how talented, wise, pleasant, or available they may be. Rev. Bill Yeager, former pastor in Modesto, California, taught that all members are to be FAT (faithful, available, and teachable), but leaders must be FATTER (faithful, available, teachable, tithers, evangelists, and disciplers).

    b. *Abilities*: The question is not whether they are talented people in general, but do they have the ability to perform well at the position they'll need to play for the good of the team? Sometimes the most capable people are not needed, because someone else is already doing what they would be excellent at. This makes one or the other redundant.

c. *Gift-mix:* This brings in the unique spiritual aspect of church ministry. The Scriptures teach us that the Lord will provide all the gifts necessary to accomplish in his church what he wants done. Does your church give its members spiritual gift inventories? Does leadership seriously consider the gift mix needed for each team as recruitment begins?

d. *Personality:* Every team is best served by a mixture of personalities. We need an analytical person to ensure that all the details are covered. We need at least one person who is sanguine to keep a sense of humor in the group and prevent a funereal atmosphere from developing. We need a driver, a choleric, to keep the team focused on goals and objectives. Along with these key components must be a group of thinking and willing followers. These phlegmatics are probably the ones who will do the bulk of the work.

e. *Willingness to cooperate:* The members of the team must buy into the philosophy, values, and convictions of the leaders and be convinced of their integrity, competency, and direction. When this is no longer true, they should get off the bus. I have found myself in situations where it became apparent I was on the wrong bus. After making every attempt to alter the direction and challenge leadership in an appropriate manner, it became obvious that it was time for me to get off the team. There is no shame in this. Teams must have players who fully buy in.

2. The *goal* is clear and communicated repetitiously.

The absence of measurable goals leaves any team wallowing in ambiguity and pious intentions. Can every member of the team articulate what they are attempting to accomplish? There is no shame in failure. Not knowing what we are trying to achieve is not only a waste of time, it is demoralizing. Absence of goals is a common denominator of half-hearted endeavor.

3. Everyone knows what *winning* looks like.

Be honest. Winning is a lot more fun than losing. But how does the team know if they win or lose? The answer is on the scoreboard (see Figure 11-a).

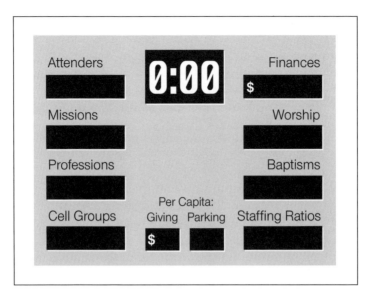

FIGURE 11-A

What numbers, facts, and other indicators are on your team's score-board? Our church recently built a gym. As we prepared to open this great new facility, our staff member in charge of sports/recreation said, "There is something important missing. We don't have a scoreboard. If, we don't get one, the basketball players will look around and say, 'Nice wood floor, great glass backboards, super facility . . . but what's the score?'"

Why is the score important?

  a. It reflects how we are doing in comparison to the competition.

  b. It gives an indication of the team effort.

  c. It forces us to understand that we will win or lose together.

  d. It makes the game exciting.

  e. It provides instant reward for hard work.

  f. It motivates us to make mid-course changes.

We have children's leagues for baseball and soccer. We have called these noncompetitive leagues to emphasize character development and the fundamentals of the games. Theoretically no one is keeping score; theoretically both teams win. But after every game each child quickly learns to ask, "Did we win?" Some view this as sad, that children must so early learn about competition. Sad or not, it is a reality. If games without the hope of winning are meaningless, then how much more so is life in the real world. Each team has freedom to define what winning looks like—but all effective teams desire to win.

4. Roles are clearly defined. All the players know their position and how it relates to the rest of the team.

In children's soccer, it is fun to watch their first couple of games. As the ball is put in motion *all* the kids run straight to it. What you end up with is a cluster of children swarming a ball that you cannot even see from the sidelines until the strongest and biggest kid in the mass of small humanity comes bursting out from the huddle momentarily kicking the ball, only to have the ball swarmed into inertia once again.

This is not how soccer is to be played. In time they quickly learn (though not always happily) that some must move away from the ball in order to receive the pass or be prepared for defense. This requires maturity and a comprehension of the game.

Not everyone can handle the ball. But everyone can contribute to winning. The best teams do not necessarily have the best individual players.

The task of the coach is to make certain all the players truly understand why and how this role is vital to success. Once that is accomplished, the players will work diligently to develop the requisite skill sets to play their position with excellence. They will also find fulfillment in what they are assigned to do.

Effective teams do *not* allow players to assign themselves whatever role or position they choose. Some players do not understand this. They wish to do only what is fun for them. They will need to be benched.

5. Every player is essential.

There are certainly less glamorous roles. Most youth would rather pitch than play right field because pitching ensures that they will have the ball in their hands much of the time. But all it takes is a fly ball to pass over the head of the right fielder in the bottom of the last inning for the game-winning single to drive home the irrefutable fact that there are *no* unimportant positions. If it were truly nonessential, there would not be such a position.

Some positions receive more attention and even more pay. But effective teams do an above-average job of communicating how vital each person is. Furthermore, the team members actually believe that what they do is critical for winning.

6. A timeline (or clock) is visible.

This clock can be temporal or eternal. But a clock must exist to give urgency to the effort.

Some organizations use several clocks: short-term (annual) goals; long-range goals (3-10 years); retirement goals; and "long-range retirement" goals (which stretch into eternity). But whatever the clock, there are several things we know about it:

a. It is a running clock. It does not stop. In a basketball game, the clock stops for every foul and every time the ball goes out of bounds. Because of all the intentional fouls in the final two minutes, sometimes that part of the game lasts as long as the preceding 18 minutes.

b. The urgency of time running out prompts players to a greater effort. One often wonders why teams don't play as hard for the entire game as they do in the last few minutes.

c. The clock will run out and the game will end.

d. You don't get time back on the clock.

e. You can adjust your game during the second half to correct the mistakes of the first half. But if you always do what you always did, you'll always get what you always got.

f. Some players will perform better under the pressure of the clock than others.

7. The stakes (and rewards) are high enough to attract big-time players.

There is truth in the statement "big dreams attract big people." The task of the coach is to communicate how big the reward is for success. We don't motivate by sharing the nightmare but rather the dream. Is the end product going to be worth the pain?

8. Personal sacrifice is expected and asked for.

There are usually a number of people sitting on the bench who would like to play if the team is winning. Therefore, each player in the game is asked to give 100 percent. Players may be asked to play hurt for the good of the team. Players are asked to practice for many hours. Players will take risks. Players will be asked to give up some other activities and pleasures. Players will be asked to stay focused on what they are doing during the game. Players will be asked to forfeit financial gain and even give of their own resources.

9. Accountability is more than a word.

Too many players in the game of life give lip service to accountability. Most rebel when it becomes reality. Players on a winning team need to arrive early, work late, do without sleep, work to the point of exhaustion, and do it for a long period of time. They must be prepared to explain their behavior. The worst thing a coach can do to a player is to so devalue them as to no longer care about their effort or performance.

10. Meetings have meaning:

- Meetings are scheduled long in advance and dates kept.

- Meetings are short, beginning and ending on time.

- Meetings are not the purpose of the team (Just as the purpose of a football team is not to huddle, but to run plays).

- Meetings are not dominated by one or two people.

- Meetings follow an agenda, reflecting the progress and purpose corresponding to the established goals.

A concluding word

Leading turnaround teams is not easy. We hope that you will have found some principles in this book to assist you in the challenge. It is unlikely you will agree with everything we've suggested. Fine. Take what is helpful and go to work.

If you were to take the time to read one chapter a second time, we would recommend you choose the chapter on Courage. Ideas, concepts, and principles will all result in no change unless the leader of the team has the confidence of his calling to move ahead.

Go ahead and do what you know needs to be done. You can do it. Yes you can!

APPENDIX A

Coaching Systems for Turnaround Teams

By Daniel Harkavy

Systems are needed when we want to improve efficiencies, when we want to have consistent outcomes, and when we want to adhere to specific standards. There are many great leaders who have had a huge impact on the lives of their team members and could not tell you how they really go about it. There are some who are naturally more gifted than others at exhorting and challenging those around them to grow to new heights. In our coaching organizations, we have created a detailed plan for how we go about coaching leaders. We knew that a consistent model would be mandatory if we were going to have the greatest level of impact on the lives of those we coach.

Many of our clients are looking for ways to improve how they coach their team members. They want to enjoy more unity and commitment from their team members. They want to improve the relationships they have with key team and lay leaders. They may have been good at the discipline and mentoring process when the organization was younger and smaller, but now they struggle with the follow-through as a result of the load that comes along with growth and success. They are looking for us to help them with their skills and with creating a plan.

Here are some basic steps any leader can take to create a solid coaching plan. Identify what we in the business world call your HPO's—high pay-off activities. These are the 3 to 5 disciplines or functions that you are best at. I know that you are probably very good at more than a dozen functions that you're performing on any given day. The key here is to identify the activities that you excel at. These are the activities that juice you up the most; they energize you and really give you maximum fulfillment. Coaching your key team members and lay leaders had better be on that short list if you're going to be a turnaround team leader.

- *Create your list of team members.* As the leader of a church with 100 or more members, you will most likely have two lists of team members.

  Your first list will have paid staff members on it. Which 3 to 5 key members need one-on-one coaching so they are better equipped to lead and coach those who are the players on their teams?

  Your second list will be your lay leaders. This list is critical. In order for your church to experience real turnaround, the hearts and lives of your members are going to need to experience turnaround—from their old life of being self-centered to their new life of being Christ-centered.

  This is how Gene and I became friends. He added me to his lay leader list. He began the process of coaching and advising me in my life. He went beyond disciplining me in the basic assurances of my faith and coached me in my parenting, marriage, and business circumstances.

  Who are the players most committed to the mission? Which members have the most potential for growth? Which players have demonstrated the most significant leadership characteristics? Write down the 5 to 10 key individuals that you are feeling led to coach. Pray over the list and write out how you think you can help each of them. Whom do you see them becoming?

- *Build your model.* I encourage your to use our Core4 model to its fullest. If you're creative and want to lay down your own track, go for it. Start off by identifying the core areas of competency or maturity that you're looking for in a coachee. Create a "scorecard." It might look something like this:

Name	Maturity	Strengths	Weaknesses	Action Plans
John J.	5/10	Leadership & Teaching	Attendance	Study on Fellowship
Steve S.	7/10	Connects with other men. (Men's Ministry?)	Unsure	Spend more time with him in Q1 2004
Rod F.	8/10	Servant hood and very handy	Temper	Confront him on this by 2-28-04
Wayne W.	Unsure	Administration	Unsure	Spend more time with him in Q1 2004

◆ *Allocate the time.* The next step in creating your plan is to define how much time you want to spend intentionally coaching your team members. Our model is very simple and has proven to be very effective since its inception in 1996.

◆ *The first coaching session.* The first one-on-one coaching session, which lasts for two hours, focuses on the big picture. Here you will want to really connect at a deeper level. Use this time to get to know your team members. What excites them, frustrates them, energizes them, and worries them? What struggles are they having today and most importantly, who do they see God calling them to be? We use the Life Plan Tool© for this. In Proverbs 20:5, we are told that the plans of a man's heart are deep waters, but a man of understanding draws them out. A man of understanding is a man of wisdom. A wise man knows what plans and purposes God has laid at the very depths of his heart.

The problem of today is that we have too many people going to school, studying extensively, and working diligently on plans that do not reside in their hearts. These plans were birthed and reside in their heads. If our plan for our life lives in our head, then we live a life with no real passion or conviction. A key ingredient for coaching success is that the coach and the team member must be operating from the heart as well as the head. If there is no heart, there can be no life changes or real impact.

Champions play from the heart. "He has heart." "What he lacks in talent, he makes up for with heart." We have all heard the heart sayings. Look in God's Word; there are quite a few verses on the heart. God knows that the key to our leadership success is our heart; it is there that he resides. You as a leader and turnaround coach must have heart, because the battle is going to be brutal and, at times, impossible if you're not operating from the heart.

The first session ends with the team member committing to completing his Life Plan on a specific date at a specific location. They must work through it in one full-day setting at a location that is free from any distractions and allows them to be creative.

What do you need for success in developing your Life Plan?

- The Life Planning tool

- Your Bible

- Your journal or a blank pad of paper

- A location that allows you to really connect with Christ, free from any interruptions

- No cell phone, pager, or e-mail.

- Water and food, if needed

Some helpful ideas our clients have shared with us:

- Go to a park and sit alongside the river for the day.

- Go to the beach and find an unpopulated cove or bluff.

- Go to a quiet lodge and sit by the fire for the day.

- Bring your running or walking shoes and take a midday break to refresh your mind.

- Challenge a friend to complete it as well. Meet with your friend early in the morning on the appointed day to pray for each other before each heading out on your own.

- Rent a hotel room for the day and have your spouse join you for dinner. Share your Life Plan with your spouse and take your marriage to new depths as you discuss your dreams and hopes for the years ahead.

Your Coaching Tools

You need to keep a folder for each team member.

The left side includes

- the coaching schedule
- the team member survey or questionnaire
- the Coaching Agreement

The right side includes

- Copies of all the member's action plans
- Tools

Your Coaching Process

- Questionnaire
- Calling, giftedness or behavioral assessment
- Any and all project lists, plans or goals
- A two-hour session ending with the Life Plan as the primary Action Plan
- Hourly sessions monthly or thirty-minute sessions every other week focused on the areas of growth desired, challenges being experienced and opportunities that lay ahead.

Every session includes:

- Prayer
- A complete action plan review with new target dates for any missed and still desired actions

- The creation of new action plans, if the team member is up to speed and prepared to continue moving forward

- Listening to the Holy Spirit for guidance

By following this type of a process, you will have an intentional and very effective system to lead your team members through turnaround.

APPENDIX B
IMPLEMENTING CHANGE

Ten Lessons of the Cluttered Garage

By Gene Wood

"But now you also, put them all aside: anger, wrath, malice, slander, and abusive speech from your mouth. Do not lie to one another, since you laid aside the old self with its evil practices and have put on the new self who is being renewed to a true knowledge according to the image of the One who created him. . . . And so, as those who have been chosen of God, holy and beloved, put on a heart of compassion, kindness, humility, gentleness and patience. . . . And beyond all these things put on love, which is the perfect bond of unity (Colossians 3:8-10, 12, 14).

Thirteen years is the longest we've lived in one house. Our life had been one of constant mobility. We moved from Oregon to Texas to Pennsylvania to Ohio. In fact in some of those locations, we moved multiple times, to a larger apartment or bigger house. Whatever the reason, we moved a lot. Then we came to California 13 years ago. We moved into our home and stayed. Do you know how much junk a family of five can accumulate in 13 years?

Stuff on shelves stacked to the rafters. Stuff in boxes crammed into every closet and enclosure. Stuff on top of the ceiling joists, stuff on the walls, exercise equipment, lawn tools, rough lumber, old paint cans. You know the stuff!

One day Carol said, "Enough." My assignment was to order a large trash container for the next Saturday. Early that morning she began sorting. The junk sat in one pile, waiting to be tossed into the trash container. Things thought worthy of being salvaged sat in another pile.

For the next four hours, I hauled stuff to the trash container. During this time, I came up with ten lessons of the cluttered garage.

1. We can gather a large amount of useless junk no matter how clean we think ourselves to be. Both my wife and I consider ourselves to be "tossers." We are not victims of the Depression. As have many boomers, we've enjoyed a life of continual increase and abundance. We don't fear the "big one" (earthquake). We're optimistic about our future. So how did we accumulate all this stuff? The answer is one small box or article at a time. One box every month for 13 years means 156 boxes of stuff. That's nearly enough to fill a small storage shed. The basic principle here is that stuff grows.

2. A time must be set aside to clear out the old stuff. We had discussed cleaning the garage for months. Both agreed it was a necessary step. But until a promise was made to order the container and schedules were mutually cleared to be present for the work, nothing got done. The principle here is that stuff accumulates until a time is put on the calendar to remove it.

3. A provision must be made so that cleaning out the old is feasible. Theoretically, we could have removed most of the articles in the normal weekly rubbish pickup. In our city they will take as many garbage cans as you fill. Some items would need to be taken apart or broken into pieces. Theoretically, that could have been done week by week. Practically, that would never happen. The stuff simply was not inconvenient enough to merit spending minutes or hours each week, to say nothing of the energy it took, to fit everything into garbage cans. When all we had to do was walk 30 feet to the large container and throw it over the edge, we were willing to do it. The principle here is that we must have a plan for discarding the old.

4. There are probably *more* things cluttering our lives than we think. We planned to order the medium-size container. Fortunately, the company we worked with was out of that size for the weekend, so they brought us the next larger size. Good thing. When they came to pick it up three days later, our discarded treasures were showing over the top of the container. The principle here is that there is much in our lives that we won't miss if it goes away.

5. Cleaning out the old is best done with another person. This gives accountability. We are forced to ask and answer the key question: "Do I really need this?" Having another objective person working along side of us also provides balance. We don't want to throw away everything! Some things do serve a purpose.

6. Establish rules to help govern what goes and what stays. As we worked to clean out our garage, we agreed upon a general rule of thumb. Things that go back to childhood and beyond (given to us by parents) stay. They can be tossed later, but they are impossible to replace once gone. Likewise, things that any of our three children may wish from their childhood were kept. An additional rule of thumb was that if it has not been used in six months get rid of it. Of course rules can be broken, but they do provide guidelines and make decision making easier.

A drifter appeared one day on an Oregon farm looking for work. The farmer handed him an axe, showed him a huge pile of tree limbs, and instructed him to begin chopping. At the end of the day the farmer was amazed to find the entire pile of limbs collected over years had been cut into pieces of firewood. Impressed with the man's work ethic, he gave him a bonus over and above the agreed upon hourly wage and begged him to stay around.

The next day the farmer felt bad about the backbreaking work the drifter had performed the day before and decided to take it easy on him. He said, "Why don't you stay here under the shade tree and just make two neat piles. Put the smaller pieces from yesterday in the kindling pile and the larger pieces in the second pile."

At noon the farmer returned with a container of cold water and lunch. He found the new hire sitting thoroughly exhausted, sweat dripping down his forehead, his head in his hands.

"What's the matter?" asked the farmer. "After yesterday I figured this would be simple for you."

The drifter grunted, "It's all these decisions. They're killing me!"

The primary reason we do not get rid of worthless junk is our unwillingness to make decisions. To clear out the old to make room for the future, we must adopt some rules of thumb and be willing to make a few mistakes.

7. Ask yourself, "Why have we kept this?" Is this item in my garage for functional or emotional reasons?

8. The process forces us to consider how much things have changed over the years. Some items in our garage represented a major purchase when we bought it, but the same item today would be an inconsequential purchase, an irrelevant purchase, or one that was important for another stage of life but unnecessary today.

9. Promise yourself a reward once you've finished the task. In our case, my wife bribed me by promising I could buy the bike I had wanted for a long time.

10. Be thankful the Lord has blessed you in such a manner that you have much to toss. What a sad thing to travel through life and have no significant memories, shared accumulations, or remnants of achievements gone by.

APPENDIX C

Sample Church Covenant for Staff Relationships

In Regards to Philosophy and Structure of Staffing

I have seen and understand the charts describing the philosophy of staffing and lines of communications (see figure C-2) at Grace Church. My agreement to be employed at Grace is also my agreement to support and abide by such policy. (Any hesitations I may have are discussed at the time of signing and initialed accordingly.) I will explain the structure to others as need may arise.

In Regards to Personal Holiness and Practice

I will strive to meet the qualities and standards given for church leadership in Titus 1 and 1 Timothy 3. In addition, I will give careful consideration to areas of questionable behavior. I will resolve such matters on the basis of two questions:

1. Could my behavior cause a weaker brother to stumble (1 Corinthians 8; 9:19)?

2. If everyone in the church did what I do, would I wish to belong to this church (1 Timothy 4:12)?

In Regards to Staff Relationships

1. I will covenant to guard my words (James 3).

2. I will covenant not to be guilty of triangling, that is, speaking about Party A to Party B so as to violate the principle of Matthew 5:23-26.

3. I will covenant not to be guilty of listening silently to people complaining or gossiping about another without insisting that they go to that person, and then confirming they have done so. Such silent listening violates the spirit of Matthew 18:15-20.

   a. I will not *imply consent by my silence.*

   b. I will inform them I cannot listen, but will gladly go with them to seek reconciliation or restoration.

   c. If an accusation is made of sin or gross injustice, I will give them a reasonable period of time to confront the offending individual. Then I will check to see that they have done this.

4. I will covenant not to judge the motives of another (Romans 14:1-12; 1 Corinthians 4:1-5).

5. When offended, I will go quickly to the offending party to seek reconciliation (Matthew 5:18; Ephesians 4:26-27).

In Regards to a Process of Grievance

1. I covenant to pray about my hurt or anger to determine whether it is appropriate or inappropriate.

2. I covenant to then speak with the offending party if my feelings are appropriate.

3. Should I not find reconciliation forthcoming, I covenant to ask my supervisor to sit with me to seek a resolution. If that is not effective, I will seek the counsel of the senior pastor.

In Regards to Grievance with the Senior Pastor

1. I covenant to go to him quickly before speaking with others.

2. If satisfaction is not forthcoming, I covenant to notify him of my dissatisfaction. He will then set up a meeting with one or two elders and himself to further air the grievance.

3. If that step does not find reconciliation, and I am still not satisfied with the results, I covenant that I will request the pastor to reserve a spot on the elder agenda in which I can plead my case.

   Note: I understand that the Elder Board at Grace Church is the final body for resolution for all matters of dispute.

4. I understand that voicing grievances in public to garner support for my cause will result in my termination.

5. I further understand that voicing my concern and following the prescribed guidelines of this covenant will ensure the senior pastor's full cooperation in assisting me in locating a desirable and suitable new position of ministry should satisfactory resolution be found impossible and relocation be determined necessary.

Signature _____ Date _____

PHILOSOPHY OF STAFFING AT GRACE

A. In the 1990's culture in North America, a church staff member is a vital ingredient in local church life — so vital that most would agree he/she should meet the qualifications of a church officer.

B. The New Testament refers to only two officers in the church. They are elders (Titus 1) and deacons (1 Timothy 3).

C. The contemporary church staff, however, does not fit neatly under the category of deacons, but seems to belong under the heading of pastor/elder.

D. Despite argumentation to the contrary by some, one cannot make the case that there is always a plurality of overseeing pastors in every New Testament congregation. In truth, logic appears to indicate there can only be one overseeing pastor. Every known *living organism has no more than one head.*

While in Dallas, Texas, teaching at Southern Bible Institute (a training school for black pastors), Dr. Reed, Dean of Students, shared a great insight with me. We were discussing church policy and organization. He observed: "You know something, Gene, if you go out in the back yard and see your dog has two heads, you're probably gonna shoot that animal. That's no dog . . . that's a monster."

God is the head of his universal church (Colossians 1:18). He is the Father head of the Trinity. Every home is to have one head (Ephesians 5:23). Every animal in all of the Lord's creation has no more than one head. Every human being is created to have one head. And God has ordained one overseeing undershepherd for each local body (Acts 20; 1 Peter 5). It appears to be one of the laws of God's creation to allow for smooth functioning of a dynamic living organism.

E. The church staff might reasonably be viewed as an *extension of the pastoral office.*

This concept affects one's attitude and choices in the selection of staff personnel. If each staff member was viewed as simply "another pastor," then each should possess all the qualifications that are sought in a senior pastor. These would include appropriate academic credentials; requisite experience; gifts such as administration and teaching; desire for the office, and so on.

One major difficulty with staffing "clones" is that such individuals quickly become frustrated within their required job descriptions. They would be limited in the opportunity to utilize their spiritual gifts and be forced to function much of the time in areas of weakness.

The other choice we have is to view the church staff as *an extension of the senior pastor.* In this case, the staff members are selected, not because they are like the senior pastor, but because they are *complementary to him* — that is, their gifts, interests, passion, and even personality complements the pastor's weaknesses or abilities.

The goal in the *jigsaw philosophy* of staffing is to, whenever possible, avoid frustration and allow each member of the team to serve a large share of the time in those aspects of ministry that are fulfilling and effective without falling all over one another. The hope is that this will produce *results for the body and contentment for the staff members.*

F. With this philosophy, church staff are selected on their perceived ability to complement one another in ministry.

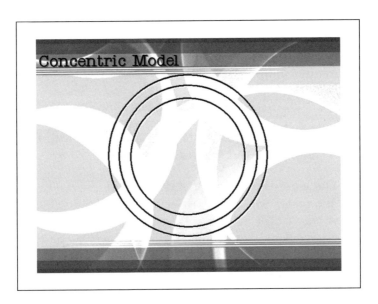

FIGURE D-1

Assumes the senior pastor is perfectly rounded, as is each staff member; they are to expand the sphere of ministry.

LINES OF COMMUNICATION

(Hebrews 13:17; 1 Peter 5:1-4; Acts 20:28)

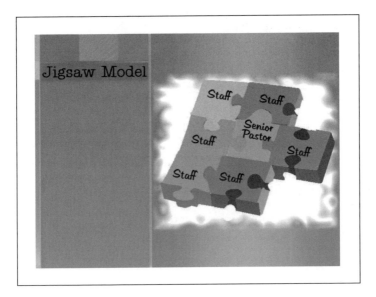

FIGURE C-1

Assumes the senior pastor has strengths and weaknesses; he attempts to build the staff around those.

Note 1: The congregation votes on whether to call the senior pastor and whether to dismiss him.

Note 2: The congregation ratifies lay elders annually.

Note 3: The senior pastor hires staff and sets salaries with Elder Board approval. He also has the prerogative of dismissal.

Note 4: The elders have agreed to delegate administration of all staff matters to the senior pastor for day-to-day operations. This, of course, must be within budget restrictions and guidelines established by the elders. This agreement is voted on annually by the elders and the motion entered into the minutes.

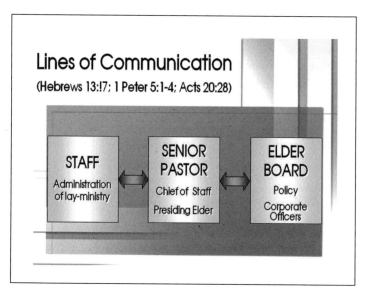

FIGURE C-1

Philosophies of Staffing

♦ Assumes the senior pastor is perfectly rounded, as is each staff member; they are to expand the sphere of ministry.

♦ Assumes the senior pastor has strengths and weaknesses; attempts to build the staff around those.